From
Stress to Success

Faster EFT
(Emotionally Focused Transformations)

Kim J Jewell

Foreword by *Robert G. Smith*

Copyright © 2012 Kim J Jewell

All rights reserved.

ISBN:
ISBN-13: 978 - 1484812136

DEDICATION

This book is dedicated to my amazing children,
Michail, Katija and Curtis,
for their patience, joy, heartache and
unconditional love.
They are my
greatest teachers.

It is also dedicated to you, the reader, for
having the courage to start your
journey to wellness and wholeness by
purchasing this book and jumping in.
It is my deepest wish that when you finish this
book you take with you the
missing piece of the puzzle that has kept you
trapped and which can no
longer hold you back.

"Memories buried alive never die,
They just show up in bigger, uglier shoes."
Robert G. Smith

"The way you talk about yourself and your life -
your story - has a great deal to
do with what shows up in your day-to-day
experience.
Your thoughts create filters through which you
view your life.
If you think of yourself as a victim, you filter all
that happens to you through the
lens of DDT (Dreaded Drama Triangle) and you
find plenty of evidence to
support that viewpoint.
That's why the orientation you adopt is so
important: it exerts a powerful
influence on your life direction."
David Emerald

Table of Contents

ACKNOWLEDGMENTS 1

Disclaimer 3

FOREWORD 7

Before We Begin 15

What is Faster EFT? 19

How Faster EFT Can Help You 25
    Stress Relief 26
    Self Image 27
    Emotional Wellbeing 28

The Belief System of Faster EFT 30
    Birth Sets the Stage 31
    Perceptions and Coping Skills 32
    Experiences and Self-Identity 33
    Why: Doctrines of Belief 33

Understanding How we have Problems 36
    Beliefs 37
    Triggers / Anchors 41
    Feelings 50

The Filing System of the Mind 53
    Our Unconscious Mind 54
    The Amygdala 56
    Reticular Activating System 59

Two Models of the World 65
Being at Cause or A Child's View of the World............ 66
Being at Effect or The Emotionally Mature View of the World.. 70

The ART of Change 73
ART of Change Questions... 77
What you don't want.. 77
What we do Want... 81
The Future.. 84

Memories and the Trance State 87
What is Real?... 87

Why Do We Tap 91

How to Tap Faster EFT Style 98

Faster EFT Tapping Techniques 112

Case Studies 125
Case Study I.. 125
Case Study II... 129
Case Study III.. 132
Case Study IV.. 134

ACKNOWLEDGMENTS

I am eternally grateful to *Robert G. Smith* for the time, hard work, dedication and passion in putting together this incredible modality that has allowed so many to break free from their personal prisons.

I am also grateful to so many people who have been a part of writing of this book and supporting my work.

My children, Katija, Michail and Curtis for their encouragement, support, inspiration and patience. I extend a heart full of gratitude and love to my friend and fellow practitioner, ***Vee***

Evans, for her contributions, editing and the hours spent working with me and not allowing me to avoid my issues. My dear friends whom have loved me, believed in me and supported me in life and this process, *Debra and Ron Redman. Kim Ryder and Gary Masters* for the ongoing love, support as well as the all the editing, spelling corrections and the kind and gentle process.

Disclaimer

*The information found in this book, **From Stress to Success with Faster Emotionally Focused Transformation (Faster EFT)** is provided only as general information and is intended to be educational in its nature. All the ideas, techniques, instruction, information and advice addressed in this book are for the purposes of self-help and are to be used entirely at your own risk.*

The information contained in this book, including the introduction to Faster EFT, is not intended to suggest that Faster EFT can be used to diagnose, treat, cure or prevent any disease or psychological disorder. Faster EFT is not a substitute for medical or psychological treatment. Reading about or using the techniques in this book and using the Faster EFT techniques on yourself should not replace any form of health care from medical/psychological professionals. For long-standing or severe emotional medical physical or psychological problems one should seek advice from your medical practitioner or health professional.

You, the reader, agree to accept and assume full responsibility to any and all risks associated with reading this book and using Faster EFT as a result of it.

You understand that your choice to use Faster EFT is of your own free will and not subject to any outside pressure.

You understand that if you choose to use Faster EFT, it is possible that emotional or unresolved issues may surface which could be received as negative side effects. Emotional issues may continue to surface after initially using Faster EFT, as an indicator that other issues may need to be addressed.

Whilst **Faster Emotionally Focused Transformations** *(Faster EFT) has produced remarkable results ,the author, Kim Jewell does not guarantee any precise level of improvement in your physical, mental or emotional well-being where any specific outcome, issue, problem or illness are dependent on specific individuals and many other outside factors.*

The testimonials or stories presented in the book do not constitute a warranty, guarantee or prediction regarding the outcome of you as an individual using Faster EFT for any particular issue. While all materials and references of other resources are given in good faith, the accuracy, validity, effectiveness, completeness of any information in this book cannot be guaranteed.

The author Kim Jewell accepts no responsibility or liability whatsoever for the use or misuse of the information provided in this book.

Kim Jewell does not accept any liability for any injury, illness, loss or damage incurred by the use of, reliance on, or participation in the techniques in this book

FOREWORD

*"Tap until it's gone or until you pass out.
Either way you will wake up to a whole new world."*

— *Robert G. Smith*

Today more than at any other time in the history of humanity, people around the world are facing stresses and tensions that are beyond their control. Millions are turning to drugs, alcohol and various other addictions in a vain attempt to cope with their daily lives in the modern world...

It's seem like such a long time since I bought my first tape set of NLP (Neuro Linguistic Programming) by Anthony Robins in an attempt to find answers to my own problems. It was so interesting because it helped me to understand how the mind works. Searching for more information led me to study EFT, Gary Craig's (Emotional Freedom Technique).

This thirst for knowledge and understanding has been my driving force. Persistence has been my favorite tool and both have taken me down many roads. I found myself questioning why am I here and where am I going...

Today my mission is to help the world one person at a time, to give them the skills to change their lives and the ability to experience life to the fullest.

FasterEFT is a personal empowerment process that comes with logical understandings and powerful tools. It gives you full control of your past, future and the present moment. It gives you the ability to transform your health, relationships and the skills to conquer any obstacle that occurs in life.

It gives you the ability to accomplish more than you could imagine because you are using the power of your own mind…

As I was reading this book so many emotions were stirring. I was touched and delighted to see my many years of work summarized in such a concise way. Kim has put together a great overview of this FasterEFT magic.

Her excellent book will help you the reader to step inside the mind of the healer. It will open the door for deep inner healing and understanding. It is a great read for clients before they have a session or for those wanting to know more of the structure of FasterEFT.

Kim's knowledge and years of experience in the healing world has now shifted with FasterEFT, which has allowed her to become a very skillful practitioner. Good job Kim for helping me to spread the great news of FasterEFT.

Robert G Smith

INTRODUCTION

If you are like me, you have read countless 'self-help' books in the hope of finding that magic bullet. If on the other hand this is your first, "Congratulations!" This book is set out to help you understand why there is no "magic bullet" and that no one else can "fix" you, *except YOU*. There is a modality out there that simplifies and creates lasting change, simply and eloquently without the years of "talk" therapy. It works for all of us, from all walks of life, cultures, races, and religious beliefs. It works on basic truths and allows each person the freedom from all that holds them back.

After years of working on myself, several psychologists, counselors, self-help groups, thousands of dollars spent on self-help books, seminars, and gurus… many left me "feeling good", but none created lasting and tangible results…until I learned about the unconscious belief change techniques that I found when I literally stumbled across Faster EFT, a modality that has taken its concepts from other modalities and put them together in a way that is down to earth, simple and logical; it cuts through the years of "talk" therapy, will power, affirmations and delivers a unique and direct way to identify and change the unconscious beliefs that perpetuate stress and problems in our life.

As I watched the first couple of videos on You Tube, I found myself wondering how this guy *Robert. G. Smith* from Oklahoma had managed to create something that had taken me the better half of almost twenty- five years of self-help and constant seeking to come to a similar sort of understanding. Here he was speaking my language, stating everything that I had been learning over the last 25 years in a simple, easy to understand and effective system. It is in a form that all of us can understand, relate to and put to use in our daily life.

Of course, I plunged head first into the training provided by Robert Smith and immediately found that profound shifts were occurring in my life. Not earth-shattering revelations, but subtle changes that happened quietly and almost behind the scenes. Most of these shifts I personally hadn't noticed until someone pointed out how differently I was responding to situations and people that had in the past set off previously almost uncontrollable triggers and reactions. They were not the spontaneous healings that you often hear about with acclaimed self-help gurus but more along the lines of long-term shifts that feel as natural as never having had the problem in the first place.

Ever hear the quote "You will never be able to love another until you love yourself first"? I could never understand this, it baffled me for years and try as I may I could never understand how to unconditionally love myself. Intellectually I understood the concept, but I had never really understood how to let go of those "unforgiveable" things and events that had happened to me, nor had I been able to move past some "self sabotaging" behavior. It had not been for a lack of trying, I had worked on my "issues" for years, tried just about everything I could find… and consequently had just reinforced all the old dysfunctional beliefs and issues that I had been trying to get rid of in the first place.

Faster EFT showed me that by letting go of all the distorted perceptions, belief patterns and taking whatever feelings were involved offline and installing new, healthy imprints. I would change and change I did! The more I let go of the old perceptions and emotions the more I really started to love myself. Forgiveness doesn't mean you approve of what happened or that it should be covered up, it means releasing the impact it has on you and finding the gift that was left behind, which is often not seen because the focus was on looking at the negative.

When we love ourselves more, we don't act out of anger because we know we are the ones who will suffer in the end. When we let go of our old stories and love ourselves, people, places, events and other things no longer upset us, because we know we have the personal power to release the upsets. The controls are inside of us. When we let go and release all the pain, fear, anger, sadness, emotional traumas, the powerlessness, and the memories from our past, self-love is what is left. When we release whatever and whoever offended us, we experience more love within and are able to love others more.

Don't be fooled, while this process is simple, there is an art behind it, a need for understanding exactly how we create our problems and how to bypass that part of our brain that believes it is keeping us safe, a commitment to changing ourselves and a willingness to tap.

This book is about giving you, the reader, a better understanding of how you represent yourself in the world, how you can effectively make changes in your life and how you perceive your world. It is not meant as the be all and end all of self-help. As with anything, you will get out of it what you put in to it. If you find yourself stuck, there are countless resources to draw upon. Use them, heal yourself and in turn you'll find that others around you will be intrigued and want to know more.

Peace and love

Kim

Before We Begin

As with many things in today's society it is important to clarify a few facts before we begin. This book is an introduction to the modality of Faster EFT.

It is not intended to be a training manual and does not cover in detail the specific tools, techniques and experimental training that a practitioner gains by attending the specified training courses.

While the information contained within is helpful and gives you an understanding of Faster EFT as a whole, it is recommended that you undertake formal training before using any of the techniques on anyone other than yourself.

Disclaimer: The information in this book is for educational purposes only and represents my personal experience and opinion as a Faster EFT Practitioner. While I have never seen any adverse effects from using any of the techniques, I cannot guarantee that there will be no adverse effects.

Before following or adopting any treatment or any opinion expressed in this book, you agree that you will first discuss the treatment or opinion with a appropriate physician or therapist and that you will follow all directions precisely and heed all warnings and cautionary information.

I am a Certified Trainer in the field of NLP, a Certified Consulting Hypnotist, a Level III Faster EFT Practitioner, A Personal Success Coach, a Professional Speaker and Teacher. I am on a quest to help individuals all over the world to uncover and discover the truth of who they really are and to live to their highest potential.

Here's to the crazy ones, the misfits, the rebels, the troublemakers, the round pegs in the square holes...the ones who see things differently – they're not fond of rules... You can quote them, disagree with them, glorify or vilify them, but the only thing you can't do is ignore them because they change things...they push the human race forward, while some may see them as the crazy ones, we see genius, because the ones who are crazy enough to think that they can change the world, are the ones who do.

— Steve Jobs

1

What is Faster EFT?

So what is this thing called Faster EFT and how is it different to EFT? This book endeavors to answer those very questions. This book is more than just a quick overview of this modality. It is about helping you understand yourself at a deeper level and giving you the tools to transform your life.

Faster EFT is a simple, fast and holistic process, a powerful technique that relieves stress of all forms and transforms our unconscious hard drive. Developed by Robert G. Smith, Faster EFT is derived from various fields of study including several forms of Neuro-Linguistic Programming (NLP), Ericksonian hypnosis, Thought Field Therapy, Traditional EFT, and various other healing systems. Robert found that by combining basic traditional EFT techniques with NLP (Neuro Linguistic Programing) processes we could utilize the mind's ability to transform itself, allowing change to happen in a fast, easy and effortless way.

It is a simple process that helps you communicate with your unconscious mind in order to change old beliefs and patterns that are sabotaging your life. It is a safe and effective way to dissolve resistance to change at the unconscious level.

Founded on the premise "There are no broken people", this technique shows us that in order to have a problem one must be doing something correctly to manifest and produce the problem that is troubling us. In fact, we have become experts at producing our problems. Faster Emotionally Focused Transformation shows us how the cause of all our problems is our personal perceptions and emotions that have been buried deep inside our unconscious mind.

Faster EFT works within a structure of a system that always works. It recognizes that we all have self-adaptive behaviors that keep us aligned with what we have recorded within us, based on our experiences, values and beliefs. These behaviors that keep cropping up and creating difficulties in our lives are really just our inner programming helping us to stay in alignment with those values and beliefs. Our beliefs determine our actions and our actions determine our results!

Faster Emotionally Focused Transformation identifies our memories as the "trance" state of stress. It breaks the physical response to the stress by tapping on acupressure points, blocking the stress signals being sent from the brain to the body and allowing the body to give positive feedback to the mind, returning the client to a calmer, more relaxed state.

Permanent change is achieved as the memories and old limiting beliefs are transformed, creating a positive imprint of an outcome or new representation of the initial event. The essence of who we are changes as we lose the negative perception of our self. This is a beautifully simple yet powerful tool and is easily learned, anyone can take it and use it to support oneself with change, any time they feel stressed.

In the early 1970's co-founders Richard Bandler and John Grinder of the University of Santa Cruz in California engaged in a study of people who were able to achieve amazing results. The co-founders took what they learned from the mental processes of "exceptional" therapists Virginia Stair and Milton Erickson MID (the grandfather of Hypnotherapy) and Fritz Pearls, who created profound changes in their patients as well as with people who had recovered from terminal illness, phobias, and other life tragedies.

NLP explores the relationships between how we think (Neuro), how we communicate (Linguistic) and our patterns of behavior and emotions (Programs).

People are able to effectively change and transform the way they traditionally think and act by studying and learning from these three areas of their lives.

NLP grew from the thousands of people who were able to transform their lives in dramatic and positive ways. It is a powerful change management tool that transforms the way people think and act creating the greatest impact in both their professional and personal lives.

NLP is "an attitude and a methodology which leaves behind it a trail of techniques". ~ Richard Bandler

Emotional Freedom Technique (EFT) is a form of "psychological acupressure" - except that needles are not used. The approach relieves symptoms by tapping on various body locations. This tapping balances energy meridians that become disrupted when we think about or experience an emotionally disturbing circumstance. Typically the result is lasting and is also accompanied by positive changes in thinking.

Emotional Freedom Techniques (EFT) evolved from Thought Field Therapy which was created by US clinical psychologist Roger Callahan. Callahan discovered that stimulating acupressure / energy points lead to psychological relief for an anxious client and through experimentation he was able to discover a series of useful points. Gary Craig, who studied with Callahan, identified a comprehensive set of "all purpose" energy points that could be applied to treat any emotional problem. He called this **Emotional Freedom Techniques (EFT)** and achieved excellent results with this approach on a wide range of emotional as well as physical problems.

Robert G. Smith, who studied both NLP and EFT, noticed that by combining key points of both these techniques he discovered that instead of the (EFT) concept of psychological reversal, the *Faster Emotionally Focused Transformation* (Faster EFT) belief system states that the body's system works perfectly, there is really nothing wrong with us, we just need to go in and clean up our "hard drive".

Instead of a blockage in the meridian system, which is the EFT belief, Faster EFT believes it is a physical reaction to what the mind holds and perceives consciously and unconsciously and by aiming at the "memory, feeling or trigger", this allows us to tap on key meridian points to release the emotional charge, therefore transforming the internal representation of what the mind is holding about the issue, collapsing the trigger and healing is achieved.

2

How Faster EFT Can Help You

For many of us the journey of self discovery has been riddled with countless promises, hopes, dreams and the trying of various methods of working out exactly how and where we've gone wrong. Most give up and settle for lives filled with poor health and emotional baggage. Not having the right tools to be able to achieve the life they desire, they are left with accepting a life of emotional trauma, physical pain, compulsions and addictions or even just an empty lost feeling inside.

If you are tired of feeling overwhelmed, sad, depressed, anxious, discontented, unwell, traumatized, trapped and caught in the cycle of stress and you're ready to move beyond all that and step into the freedom that comes from letting go of all the baggage you've picked up along your journey, you've picked up the right book. If your aim is to grow as a person, to flourish and thrive, leaving the past in the past where it belongs, it's time to step into being the best you, allowing your true self to shine and live a life that is peaceful, joyful and fulfilled.

Emotionally Focused Transformation is a therapeutic tool for emotional and physical issues because of its ability to eliminate stress, fear and doubt and teaches us to focus our mind. It is a tool that once applied will allow you to step into your authentic self and live from that place of knowing who you are and where you are going. It is a fantastic tool for calming or soothing yourself emotionally, mentally and physically. There are many ways that using this wonderful modality will benefit you and the people around you.

The benefits of incorporating this methodology into your life are too numerous to list in a short amount of time. Below are a few key areas;

Stress Relief

Today's number one cause of illness is Stress. We all suffer from stress and anxiety at one level or another from time to time and it shows up in our body in a number of ways; pain, headaches, muscle tension, a pounding heart, etc. and often will have a huge impact on us physiologically as well as on our personal performance on a day to day basis. Left unchecked it often builds up leading to more serious illness.

Whether the amount of stress is small or starting to take over your life, it can be eliminated with the use of Faster Emotionally Focused Transformation.

Self Image

Most people suffer from low self-esteem and a poor self- image at some time or at some level during their life. It is when we are stuck and stay stuck, regardless of how uncomfortable it is, resisting putting ourselves forward or stepping into new areas that our life begins to spiral downward.

Self-criticism is one of the biggest causes of poor self-image and stress. That constant feeling as if you are not good enough, not clever enough, of feeling unworthy or not being accepted creates a perpetual state of stress. There are many reasons why we have developed the habit of being so self-critical, why we worry about not measuring up. When using Faster EFT the "Why" is not important, the focus is on "How do you know that you're not measuring up?" and "What would it look like if you were good enough?"

With consistent and effective use of the techniques learned here, building self- confidence and improving our self-image becomes effortless. We start to feel comfortable in our own skin and moving forward is as natural as taking a breath.

Emotional Wellbeing

Many of us are at the mercy of our emotions or not able to allow ourselves to feel our emotions for various reasons, wary of the side effects that might happen if we do. For example; "I can't let myself get angry because I will not be able to control it or what happens." Society, culture, and familial beliefs often teach us to put a lid on our emotions, teaching us to stuff them deep inside.

Emotions ranging from rage, anger, frustration, sadness, disappointment, embarrassment, shame or guilt are often shunned. These emotions trapped within our physical body and not released are often what have a huge impact on our health and our ability to perform.

Faster Emotionally Focused Transformation teaches us a safe, simple and effective way to feel, express and let go of these emotions. It allows us to think more clearly and make choices from a place of empowerment. This leads to a sense of calmness and generally results in a positive change in attitude.

Here is a list of just of few issues that others have found freedom from:

- Addictions and Substance Abuse
- Allergies
- Anxiety and Panic Attacks
- Anger Issues
- Exams
- Fear of Failure
- Fear of Public Speaking
- Financial Issues
- Greif & Loss
- Illness
- Insomnia
- Learning Difficulties
- Pain/Physical & Emotional
- Phobias
- Performance Anxiety
- Procrastination
- Relationships
- Road rage
- Self-criticism
- Stress
- Shyness
- Transition and Change
- Trauma
- Weight loss

3

The Belief System of Faster EFT

The first thing to know about Faster EFT is, that like many other modalities, it has a foundation or belief system from which all the processes are established. There are no long, involved processes that need to be learned. Most of what is needed to successfully use Faster EFT is already part of your daily life. Understanding the belief system behind the system will give you clear directions on how to transform your life. It is user-friendly and it isn't necessary to believe anything new in order to agree with the foundational beliefs of this system.

You will find the beliefs needed to work within the Faster EFT framework are true for everybody, whether you are living in the outback of Australia, a high rise in New York City, an Ashram in India or a bungalow on the beach. They work regardless of your background, your financial status, religion or race. You are not going to be asked to believe in any "new age" or any other "out there" belief system.

Faster EFT operates on the belief that all changes happen naturally in the following way: First; by taking a bad or negative feeling and removing any emotional charge from it, *(Feeling Bad)* **+ *add an*** imprint of a new perception *(Feeling Good)* **= *Collapse***. Every time there is a collapse of the bad feelings with good feelings a shift happens. Tapping is a collapsing process. It allows the release of bad feelings by firing off two emotions at the same time during the tapping process.

The following are the basic beliefs that Faster EFT are founded on:

Birth Sets the Stage

- Birth is the beginning of all our problems.

Believe it or not… every one of our problems started the moment we were born. Take a moment and think about it. Before any of us were born, an environment existed that has cultural and familial dynamics into which we enter at birth. Our parents/caregivers came together with their own very unique set of beliefs and values.

Despite the circumstances of our birth… regardless of the specifics, the environment into which we entered already had a set of beliefs and values. "They" (our parents, relatives, caregivers, siblings, teachers, and the society they live in) already had their skills, their issues and their problems before we arrived. Our mother gave birth to us and we entered the arena.

Perceptions and Coping Skills

- As an infant we are taking all of our cues from "them" (our primary caregivers). In order to survive we are dependent on them (primary caregivers) for clues to survive and thrive.

We start to develop coping skills to deal with the environment in which we are a part of. Our goal is to stay alive and we adapt to the unique events that are happening in our world. We begin to form perceptions about how and what is going on around us. With the limited capacity of an infant, our focus is on survival and we are completely dependent on our caregivers and their responses for our survival. Very quickly we learn skills to get our needs met, whether those skills are dysfunctional or not doesn't matter, it is all about survival and staying safe.

Experiences and Self-Identity

- From the experiences of our early years and the perceptions we have formed about those experiences we (the child) start to form our identity from within.

This self-identity is based solely on the child's experiences and how the child perceives the experience. As a child we often want to emulate our parents and begin modeling their behaviors with our perceptions. Every experience becomes a learning opportunity. From this identity the child begins to interact with the world. What the child learns in the early environment becomes "normal" to that set of conditions and the child looks to the world for a way to fit into that model.

Why: Doctrines of Belief

- The child then begins to ask "Why" to make sense of the world in which they live. The world responds with doctrines of belief as to why good or bad things occur.

We grow up with many beliefs coming from our family or culture that suggest the reasons for our multitude of problems and why we are "messed up". We are offered any number of doctrines to attach ourselves to in order to explain our problems and pain.

We start to take of some of these theories and use them to explain why the world is the way it is. See if you can recognize some of these theories that include but are not limited to: tradition, culture, God's Plan, the economy, sin, virus, my past, bad karma, past lives, genetics, brain chemistry, life lessons, I picked it (I choose to be born into this life), Ego.

The common theme that we see here is the perception of: "There is nothing I can do about it, it's out of my control. It's just the way it is." We are almost encouraged to give all our power away. That "they" are somehow responsible for all that is happening to us.

Faster EFT doesn't buy into any of those beliefs. It works on the premise that life is full of experiences. Within each and every person these experiences are stored in the mind/body as a reference. Based on our references and the proofs that we hold, along with the sensory stimuli such as images, feelings, and sounds and smells that act as triggers, we start to repeat patterns and in turn build more supports for our problems.

"Why?" becomes an unproductive question because it leads us on a wild goose chase, giving us more excuses and supporting our problems. Even if we knew the cause of a problem it does not solve it, it creates a new loop endlessly seeking to find the answer to "why?"

4

Understanding How we have Problems

"The significant problems we have cannot be solved at the same level of thinking with which we created them."
— *Albert Einstein*

So you think problems find you… that people, things and events outside yourself create the problems, right? If only certain things hadn't happened, or if your partner would only follow the rules, or if your boss understood you better, then you would be okay. If your partner didn't have so many issues then you wouldn't have any problems. Well, I hate to be the one to burst your bubble, but you are about to find out exactly where and how these pesky little things called problems come from: one place only… that's right… it is all about YOU, all your problems, issues, dramas, and the whole gamut comes from inside you. Now notice how strong that feeling of denial is as you find yourself wanting to contradict me… just keep reading, open your mind and find your way out of all these "problems".

Beliefs

Our reality is created by our "beliefs". Our beliefs, mostly unconscious, are the result of our lifelong "conditioning" and represent a powerful influence on our behavior. It is from our beliefs that we form attitudes about the world and ourselves, and from these attitudes we develop our behaviors.

From the moment we are born our brain is recording every event, every feeling, and every reaction, positive or negative. These experiences, our perception of the experiences and the emotions associated with them are stored in the filing cabinet of the emotional brain. This filing cabinet of the mind decides how to record and where to store the memories based on the emotional stimuli present at the time of the event. As we go through life this filing cabinet is used to access emotional responses according to the stimuli being sent through our vision, our hearing and our touch, sending a message to our physical body which results in an emotional and physical response. Have you ever noticed when you hear a song from your past, a time like high school, you experience similar feelings as you did back then?

Imagine if you saved every document you ever wrote in your computer's hard drive, everything, you haven't edited, deleted or reconfigured anything… imagine how much unproductive information you would have just lying around, creating a mess, making it difficult to sort through and find what you need… that is what most of us do with our unconscious mind. It's time to go in and clean up and defragment the old hard drive of our beliefs.

The only moment in time that is real is the present moment. It is the only time we have the opportunity to make a choice. Anything prior to that moment is "history", it does not exist anymore and we cannot change it. The only way we hold on to it is with memories. When the written word is used to record this history, it is recorded through the perception of the person recording the events. Others use photographs to record events and when viewing these photographs they view them through their own filter of perception of what actually happened.

The truth is… we never really experience that moment again, except through a *thought process in our mind… our memory*, regardless of whether we are reading it or viewing it, or feeling it, we must engage the thought process and in turn it produces an emotional response to the memory.

A classic example of this is when there is an incident that involves multiple people; during the interviewing process ... it is often found that each person involved has a different recollection as to what exactly happened. While they all witnessed the same event, it has been filtered through each person's perspective and perception leading to differences in what each saw and experienced.

So, as a young child when we experience getting "into trouble" from our parents for doing something that could be life threatening, from the child's perception they may hold the emotional belief that there is something wrong with them, dad or mom doesn't love them because they are scolding them. The parent's perception is that they are trying to teach the child how to navigate the world and stay within the parameters of the social guidelines. The parents feel they are helping their child. Who is right and who is wrong? Neither, it's just the perceptions of each. It's what the child takes away and practices over and over again that then becomes a belief about themselves.

We also engage these thought processes and perception filters on the events that are yet to come. Quite often using the experiences in our past to predict what will happen in our future. To *"rehearse"* what our actual response will be if certain things happen… still not real, just thought processes being practiced over and over.

If you have ever been "dumped" in the past, there is that constant niggle that it will happen in the present situation as well. The present moment becomes lost to that worry and "trance "about the past. We look for proofs in the situations around us to solidify our beliefs and emotions about the past and then project them on to our future. The mind is trained to seek out and search for proofs to back up our beliefs.

When we practice these same thought processes repeatedly they form pathways to the emotional part of the brain creating a smooth path for the emotions to then in turn reach our physical body and create a response. When these thought processes are practiced often enough the pathway becomes a highway with many side roads to produce the same result becoming an automated process in the unconscious mind.

It is these beliefs, often concealed in the very deepest levels of our UNCONSCIOUS MIND, that make our life what it is today and what it will be tomorrow. Bear in mind, the unconscious mind is habitual, it thinks concretely (does not differentiate between real and imagined), it is timeless and has an expanded processing capacity of thousands of events at a time at a rate averaging 4 billion bits of information per second.

"Our minds work the same way as computers and over 99% of the power of our mind is in the subconscious, the hard drive of our bio-computer."

~ Dr. Bruce Lipton

Triggers / Anchors

Our mind creates reference points for these previously described pathways, often referred to as "Triggers" or "Anchors". A "Trigger" is a sensory stimulus linked to a specific set of states of being. It is also a way to access certain states of being (i.e.; emotions, awareness, memory, etc.) at a later time. The "trigger" or "anchor" sets the stage and is connected by aspects of the event such as sight, sound and/or feelings. It is also known as the *stimulus response conditioning*. When we are dealing with behavior, a 'trigger" is when something happens or someone does something and you suddenly have an automatic reaction.

These triggers are linked to both positive and negative emotions. The negative triggers show up and you have an automatic reaction... sometimes saying or doing something that hurts yourself or someone else and you're left without understanding why it happened.

Triggers can be in the form of words, something we hear, feel, taste, or smell. They can be a phrase spoken, a touch, or an object. There are both positive and negative triggers. When fired off these triggers will set off a chain reaction in our brain leading to an emotional response from a prior event.

For example: As a young child I loved spring. The weather is warming up, the sun is shining and when my father or brothers would mow the lawn, the smell of freshly cut grass would evoke the feeling that all is right in the world. They mowed the lawn every week from spring to autumn. This sense of wellbeing was experienced many times and recalled as often. I grew up and moved away, lived in the city and didn't have a lawn, yet during the spring and summer months others would mow their lawns and I would recall that time in my life and my body would flush with that sense of wellbeing. Now, every time I smell freshly cut grass I get a warm and fuzzy feeling that spreads throughout my body leaving me with the same "All is right with the world" feeling.

Note: There was nothing happening to me to create the feeling of wellbeing other than the "trigger" of the smell of fresh cut grass. I had entered a "trance state" called memory and the thoughts produced a feeling in my body.

It is important for us to understand that the human body is made up of a subtle energy system that we normally do not experience through our five senses. With just a mere thought, this energy travels throughout our bodies following specific pathways known as channels or meridians and creating internal reactions within us. The entire system is connected, so the flow of life travels from one meridian to the next, circulating through out the whole body. We have all heard about this system in one form or another… you may have heard it being called Chi by the Chinese, in India they call it Prana, the Japanese call it Ki, the Hawaiians call it Mana and in Quantum Physics it is known as energy.

Any time we experience trauma, stress, negative words and any number of other factors it affects the flow of this energy. When this happens, the amygdala (the primitive brain) records and stores the information "How to react in the future" within the neurological system. This information is stored in both the mental and physical bodies.

"Research shows that the brain does NOT know the difference between a real and a perceived or imagined event". ~ *Dr. Anees Sheikh, Professor of Psychology at Marquette University*

The unconscious mind knows and utilizes both positive and negative energies as references. It uses them to build and maintain the structure of beliefs that support past events. *The root of any of our problems originates from the meanings we give to an experience or situation, or the references we use and the internal process that occurs within us during the event.* It's how we look at it and then produce it.

Have you ever seen a hamster get on the wheel in their cage and go around and around? It runs at a speedy pace and looks as though it believes it is going somewhere. This is similar to what we do with our problems. Our mind wants to keep us safe and we think by somehow going over and over the problem we will be able to work out a solution. Yet the opposite is true, all we do is create more pathways to the same issue.

It starts with an internal reference "a belief or perception". We have an event that triggers a response within ourselves creating a conscious or unconscious reaction. From here we make judgments about the situation, leading to more references "beliefs or perceptions", and other emotional reactions, we start to feel the urge to avoid, escape or "numb out" the feeling which in turn creates even more internal references and around and around we go.

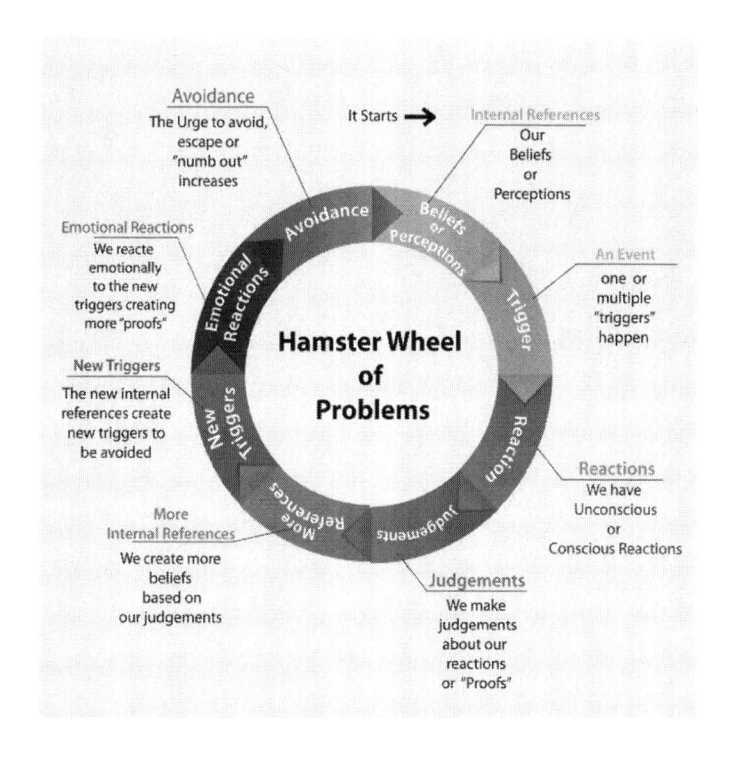

Hamster Wheel of Problems

- **It Starts → Internal References**: Our Beliefs or Perceptions
- **An Event**: one or multiple "triggers" happen
- **Reactions**: We have Unconscious or Conscious Reactions
- **Judgements**: We make judgements about our reactions or "Proofs"
- **More Internal References**: We create more beliefs based on our judgements
- **New Triggers**: The new internal references create new triggers to be avoided
- **Emotional Reactions**: We reacte emotionally to the new triggers creating more "proofs"
- **Avoidance**: The Urge to avoid, escape or "numb out" increases

As infants and children one of the primary purposes of our mind was to keep us alive. When events happened out of our control our mind was busy finding ways for us to perceive how we could stay safe. Again, based on the perception we held of our world in the moment. The problem comes when the unconscious mind is using these old outdated references to structure beliefs, they are references of a very young mind without the ability to reason. These beliefs are then carried forward as we become adults and are no longer suitable for our present circumstances, yet we are operating from that unconscious set of values and beliefs from so long ago. We experience the methods the unconscious may have once used or may have been the best choice at another time. Where the problem lies is that there is no guarantee the "protection " the mind is trying to provide is in the individual's best interest at the present moment.

As we get older, most of the initial events that created the references and pathways of our beliefs and triggers are long forgotten by the conscious part of our mind. Some of these events appear to be so subtle that people do would not believe they would affect them as adults.

It is not until we address the emotional, trance state (memories) and take any unresolved emotions offline and flip the way that we hold them in our subconscious (our internal representation) to a positive imprint that the issues dissolve and allow us to live in peace.

It's also important to note that the primary years are not the only time we create imprints in our minds about events. Anytime a person perceives a life-threatening event, the primitive part of the brain is activated in order to ensure our survival. Each time it is activated it creates an imprint from which it will draw on if events appear the same or have been clustered together.

Let's say as an adult you witness or are involved in a tragic event like, a car accident. Based on what you tell yourself about the event you either react with resilience or you replay the trauma over and over trying to ask the old "why" or "what if" questions. This replaying of the incident re-traumatizes you each time you replay it. Keeping in mind that the subconscious cannot tell the difference between what's real and what's imagined, each time you re-experience the "feelings" around the accident your mind is creating new pathways. Before you know it, you are feeling anxious before you get into a car or go and drive somewhere.

You then become focused on the anxiety you are experiencing, and start to replay that and before long you are starting to have panic attacks at the very thought of getting into a car or going on a trip. It doesn't stop there either… when we allow our self judgment to run unnoticed… let's say we've been clumsy in the past, and each time we attempt to do something, that little inner critic steps up and reminds us of how clumsy we are… this repetitive process will eventually make it's way to the subconscious mind and then it becomes an automated program or belief structure.

For example, someone learning to drive a car has a high expectation of how well they should do and how it should play out. They have spent years watching others drive and perceive that it is a simple process. When it's their turn to learn to drive, they get in the car and as there are so many processes that they have to pay attention to in the beginning and they naturally make a few mistakes. The inner critic pipes up and tells them that they are a bad driver. Each time they get into the car, they find themselves making some small mistake and confirming what they already knew… that they are a bad driver. They then start to own this label and repeat it to everyone that gets into the car with them. Faster EFT refers to this as rehearsing the problem.

They have the emotions and the proofs attached to the belief and if they continue affirming to themselves and others what a bad driver they are, new neuro pathways for this belief pattern start to form. It gets stored in the filing cabinet of the mind and each time the driver gets into the car the mind will pull up a reference as to why they are a bad driver. When we are able to change how we react to such events stored in the filing cabinet of the emotional brain, we change our internal software, and effectively remove the urges to "numb out" or tranquilize ourselves, thus interrupting our habitual cycles of trauma, stress or anxiety..

Talk therapy and other modalities often think that there is a prior event, something that happened to "cause" our behavior pattern or symptoms and one must go in and examine this "prior event" with a fine-toothcomb. The truth is, the "original event" is history and no longer real. Rehashing it will not serve any purpose.

What shows up here in the present moment is the "memory of the event" and the belief about the world and ourselves. At the time of the "original event" our mind was busy creating and internalizing self-protective beliefs. Then as time progressed, we attracted people and or circumstances to reinforce these beliefs. Fast forward to today; we are influenced and directed not only by the beliefs of the original event but all the other events that mimic the initial event in some way.

It is these old beliefs that are directing and limiting our present experiences and so, when you look at it this way, you can see it doesn't matter whether the belief started 20 years ago or 20 minutes ago, the effects and outcomes are the same.

Feelings

Thoughts and feelings come to our awareness in flashes; they arrive without any effort on our part. All these feelings and thoughts originate in the unconscious mind. Things like depression, anxiety, eating and compulsive disorders, phobias, obsessive thought, and all our unwanted behavior, they all begin in the unconscious mind.

These persistent, uncomfortable feelings have a strong influence on our thoughts, decisions and actions. They are what lies underneath compulsions, fuels addictions and gives weight to depression.

Since they begin in the unconscious mind, trying to consciously fight or change these feelings becomes an endless loop of a battle. We can eliminate these negative feelings permanently, at their root, by changing and correcting the information stored in the unconscious.

By slowing down the perception of time, we can then clearly see the pictures that underpin the thoughts and feelings. We can now get a better grasp of the images that influence every waking moment. In using this process we can heal past trauma, abuse, or neglect. This process, <u>Metaphor Therapy</u>, helps locate unconscious parts of the self, and once found we can reintegrate them back into the psyche. This restores qualities or characteristics that we thought we had lost. This process generates a new sense of wholeness, restoration and strength. The inner healing promotes outward change. The change leads to more control, satisfaction, acceptance of self and achievement. Restoring the lost qualities of the self gently always helps to quiet the mind and fill the soul.

Perception, thought and understanding are filtered through the unconscious part of our mind; the unconscious forces of the inner mind rules our existence.

The good news is we can now go inside and find out how we internally represent our world in our unconscious mind. As we discover consciously the internal world it allows us to change the external world.

Bernie S. Siegel, M.D., author of Love, Medicine, & Miracles says *"the light is better in our conscious minds, but we must look for healing in the dark subconscious."*

5

The Filing System of the Mind

"Brains aren't designed to get results; they go in directions. If you know how the brain works you can set your own directions. If you don't, then someone else will."

~Richard Bandler~

In order to resolve negative emotions (stress, anxiety, fears and phobias) we have to address and change the cause of the emotion. First it is important to understand what creates emotion. Emotions are the body's response to our internal understandings or perceptions of our external world (basically our thoughts, attitudes and beliefs).

Emotion is an internal reaction to perception. When

we experience a positive or negative emotion, the body releases certain chemicals and we feel it physically. The reaction we feel physically supports and gives meaning to the emotion which in turn impacts our mental process.

When we experience pleasant/positive feelings like love, joy, or happiness, the body produces chemicals called endorphins and dopamine that have an uplifting effect on our mental state. When we experience negative emotions, the body will produce high levels of adrenaline, serotonin and cortisol. All emotions, good or bad, are felt physically. The physical response is a "proof" that gives meaning to our memory and to the external world.

Our Unconscious Mind

Understanding the way our mind records and stores information is vital in recognizing how we have problems and how we can change the internal representation in our perceptions.

Our unconscious mind is like the hard drive on our computer. It runs programs behind the scenes that allow us to operate on a daily basis a multitude of processes that keeps our body alive. The unconscious mind stores our permanent memories, our habits and emotions are stored and is responsible for our protection, real or imagined. It keeps our heart beating, our hair growing, our organ systems running and the automatic response of drawing breath.

As infants, we are completely dependent on our primary caregivers for our survival. From the time we are born to the first nine months of our life we are at the mercy of our caregivers and everything they are feeling. Our brain has yet to develop the ego defense. Our brains are learning directly from our caregivers parasympathetic system (the emotional brain). What our parents were feeling, dealing with and making decisions about based on their perception is being directly downloaded into our emotional brain.

As we grow up we start to develop the ego defense mechanism. We start to see that we are separate from others and we start having our own perceptions, judgments, and beliefs about the world. As we grow we continue to learn and if you practice a process often enough it moves from your conscious mind to the unconscious and becomes an automatic process. Do you remember learning to tie your shoes? At first it was difficult and now it is something you do without even thinking about it.

The Amygdala

The unconscious mind records everything that happens to us between birth and the present moment. It has its own language that speaks in pictures, sounds, smells, touch and feelings. Everything that happens to us is stored in a part of our emotional brain, the primitive brain, also known as the amygdala. The amygdala looks like two almond sized shaped nuclei in the brain. It decides how to store all the input it receives and what importance it plays in our survival. All the sensory inputs that we experience are recorded and stored based on the perceptions of the individual. This becomes the blueprint for much of what we feel and think, usually unseen, as it is so deeply embedded in our personality and makes up who we think we are.

Being the filing system of the emotional brain, the amygdala flags each event with a code and stores it according to its importance on our survival. Based on the emotional reaction at the time of the initial event, the amygdala acts as a storage device and when a "trigger" happens it creates a reaction faster than your conscious mind is aware. These two little almond sized nuclei within our brain set off a lightning fast response to any emotionally significant event. This response is known as the "Fight, Flight, Freeze" response.

The amygdala is responsible for protecting us from harm by interpreting events based on the previously stored input..

When we experience painful experiences in our life they are accompanied by patterns of internal and external sensory inputs, our amygdala then creates a system of combined memory patterns that are directly related to pain. When it later recognizes any of these patterns it sets off the chain reaction alerting our organs to anticipate pain. Some of the painful experiences have been acquired through our own painful experiences in life and others we have inherited as they have been passed down through generations. The combined memory patterns then allow the amygdala on recognition to react "immediately", setting off a knee-jerk reaction- similar to a bull charging a red rag… the rag is not really a threat, but it represents one.

The amygdala reacts to emotionally charged events in many ways but the one we are focused on is the response of the sympathetic nervous system. It takes our conscious mind around 300 milliseconds to become aware of negative stimuli, it only takes 20 milliseconds for the amygdala to set off a series of events that puts our bodies on high alert for danger.

A negative "trigger" sets off a chain reaction initiating a sequence of nerve cells firing and releasing chemicals that prepares our body for running or fighting.

When our fight or flight response is activated, we tend to perceive everything in our environment as a possible threat to our survival. The very nature of the 'fight or flight' system bypasses our rational mind and we go into "attack" mode. At this point of alert we start to perceive almost everything in our world as a possible threat to our survival. In this state we are likely to see everything and everyone as a possible enemy.

This reaction was originally used to keep us alive in times of danger. Today, when we react, we find that the amygdala is being fired off more and more by the everyday stresses we face as we place more stress upon ourselves through unrealistic expectations and when reliving the past. Whether we realize it or not, each time we go back and relive in our mind our past experiences, we create stronger pathways for the reactions to run their course.

It's a bit like having more than one road to get to the final destination. Our unconscious mind is our own genie in a bottle, or Aladdin's lamp. Our every wish is its command. Not our "Conscious" wishes, the master is the unconscious which\ is neutral when it comes to expressing what we hold within… it just continues to reflect what we already hold deep in our automated processes. This is why it is so important to go in and clean up our past memories or "triggers" from the original imprints.

Reticular Activating System

Now let me introduce the Reticular Activating System, often referred to as the RAS. It is the link connecting the brain to the spinal cord and is about the size of a marble.

Its function is to point out what is important to you, like an antenna it searches and finds what 'you' believe to be true. It is believed that the RAS is the bridge that joins the mind and the body. It acts as a communication link between the two.

In any given moment we receive about two billion sensory inputs per minute and it is the unconscious mind that filters all that information and then alerts us if there is a problem. It also points out anything that is of importance to us. Think about the last time you bought a new car. Remember how when you decided on a make and model you started to notice that particular make and model everywhere, when previously you had not really noticed that particular kind car in your daily routine. It also works when someone asks you to notice how the chair feels against your back, the temperature of the room or to take notice of a certain color within eyesight. You would not have noticed any of these things if they had not mentioned them to you.

The RAS is like the control room of our mind/body system. It takes all the stimuli being received and matches it with the values and fears already stored deep in the unconscious. It works the same way with beliefs, whether about yourself or your world. If you believe you are in danger, you start to see danger everywhere. If you believe you are dumb the RAS will point out ways in which you are dumb. This programing often comes from what we have experienced in our environment and from the conditioning of our parents, teachers and the events in our lives.

The RAS acts as an auto pilot system to keep us on track based on what we have become comfortable with. If we start to make changes without first changing the original imprints in our subconscious mind it is the RAS that starts to create an uncomfortable feeling, like something is not quite right, or that something isn't working. We start to feel irritable and restless, then we give up and go back to what feels familiar. It's as if the autopilot sends out a red alert saying that we are off track from our original destination and so it corrects our course.

We are able to take charge of how we feel, how we perform and what we believe by changing our focus and changing the set point of our RAS. In order to do this we must first take any charge off the emotional imprints we already have, flip the representation of those imprints and then affirm what it is that we do want.

Faster EFT uses many references to trees and their roots. Let's consider the "supports" of any issue. Every issue in our life will have many aspects that support it. Each of these aspects is likened to a tree in the forest. Take the death of a loved one for example; you may have several issues or aspects that support the problem. (Grief, guilt, loneliness, abandonment, beliefs about what happens when someone dies, other people's reactions, etc.) These are issues are like the trees that make up the forest. As you address each of these aspects (or tree) eventually the whole forest will be cleared.

As we look at a tree, the trunk, limbs and leaves are visible to the eye and represent our consciousness. They are our problems as we see them. They are the parts of our problems that we are aware of. Basically those parts of the tree that are exposed are our current perception of our problems and successes; but the part we are not seeing is buried below the surface.

The roots are the source or life force that supports the tree (or problem).

Our unconscious mind is our root system. It's the part that knows how to walk or use a fork or knife automatically when we need to. It is the database of all our experiences and supports and maintains what we consider to be the answers to problems in our life. The unconscious mind knows the causes and all the emotions that support a problem. After repeating something (a thought or emotion with proofs to back it up) a number of times it makes it's way to the unconscious and becomes an automated program.

It's our unconscious mind that successfully produces what we are now experiencing. We use all the skills from our earlier problem solving methods as a resource for how to interact and react to our present and future issues. The only problem with this is that these resources are often founded on a child's mind, their reasoning and experiences which is not only limited but laced with the issues passed on from the primary caregivers. Our files need updating, we need to clean up and clear out the immature, irrational, illogical emotions/fears/feelings and update them to conscious, positive, and emotionally mature references.

The question then becomes "How do we upgrade these so called files if they are deep in our unconscious and we are not able to "think" our way out of them?"

This is where Faster EFT steps in and shows us a simple, easy to use technique that allows us to take these pesky imprints offline, update our filing system and create a new internal representation in our amygdala... Faster EFT is the defragmenter of our unconscious programs.

6

Two Models of the World

"We operate within two worlds. The first is the external world and the second is our internal representations (how we see it) of the external world. Pain and pleasure are the internal signals (felt in the body) that give meaning to the external world and they supervise everything we do."
~ Robert G. Smith

Understanding how we view the world is one of the first steps we take in letting go of old beliefs, imprints or negative emotions that appear to be running our lives. In this chapter we'll look at the two different ways that most of us view our worlds. While there are people that make the transition from the first model of thinking to the second model naturally, there are many more that appear to be stuck in the first model.

Being at Cause or A Child's View of the World

So what is "Being at Cause"? A cause is a force happening on an object, which puts it into motion. When an event happens it is often followed by "why did that happen?" For example, when you looked at me like that it made me feel sad. Why did you look at me like that?

As infants and children we are at the mercy of our environment. We are dependent on others for everything we need, our food, comfort and safety. These all come from someone or something outside of ourselves. We start to form beliefs around our feelings and emotions being caused by the actions of others. How our caregivers react to events often encourages and supports these belief systems. If little Johnny falls down the stairs, the parent may respond by saying "bad stairs" or "naughty stairs". The parents are implying that it is the stairs' fault that the child is hurt instead of the child understanding they played a part in their injury. Another example may be when a child becomes ill after eating a particular food, the child will "blame" the illness on the food they ate.

We then start to carry this mode of thinking into to every area of life. For example, "I got a failing grade because the teacher doesn't like me". "I'm not good at something because they laugh at me." "The reason I'm shy is because people make fun of me." As we grow up this mode of thinking that "they" are the cause of all our unhappiness is confirmed and becomes our unquestioned reality. This often compounded in the teenage years when the child is seeking its own separate identity from their caregivers. The following statements demonstrate how the thinking in the lower model of the world operates. She makes me angry. The teachers are unfair. My parents limit me. My job is stressful and that's why I'm grumpy. If you would act differently then we'd be happy. You're the reason I'm not happy. The government isn't taking care of us.

This first model of the world is a problem when a person believes that another person's actions are the cause of their emotional state. Statements and beliefs like "she makes me angry" are really a belief that another person has direct control over our emotional state. When the truth is that same behavior wouldn't necessarily make someone else angry. While other people can influence our emotions, believing that they actually have control over our emotions is a very limiting belief and view of the world. Thinking that we control someone else's emotional state or that they have control over ours is not only a huge responsibility for one to bear, but also an impossible feat.

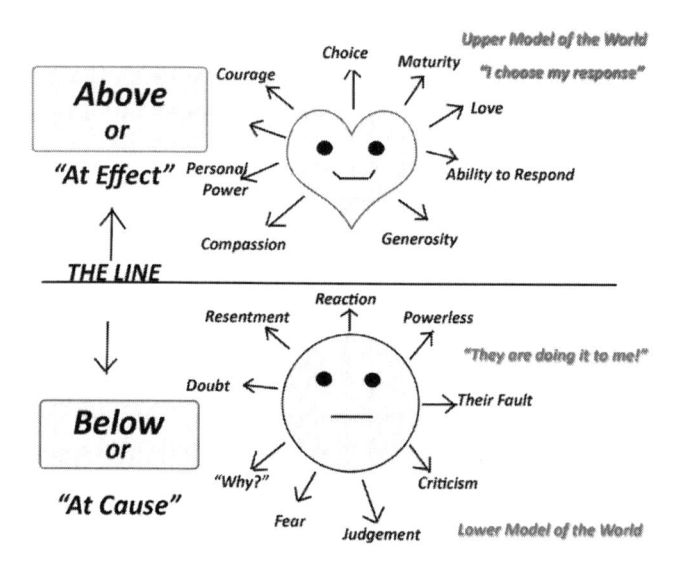

Above or "At Effect" (Upper Model of the World — "I choose my response")
- Courage
- Choice
- Maturity
- Love
- Ability to Respond
- Generosity
- Compassion
- Personal Power

THE LINE

Below or "At Cause" (Lower Model of the World — "They are doing it to me!")
- Resentment
- Reaction
- Powerless
- Their Fault
- Criticism
- Judgement
- Fear
- "Why?"
- Doubt

The other downfall of being stuck in this model of the world is that we are constantly asking "why did this happen?", it is as if miraculously once we found the root cause or the one that created the problem it would just disappear. This is another trap of this mode of thinking. We spend endless hours analyzing the "problem". We hope that by understanding "why" something happened it would solve how we are feeling about it and thus creates an endless loop. The problem is that we are powerless over people, places and things. In this model of the world we give our "power" away. We give it to "them", whoever or whatever "them" may represent.

Even if we could work out why someone said or did something, we are powerless to change them or their thinking. The inability to change others and the exterior conditions leaves the person operating in this mode with the feeling of being a victim of the circumstances. The main reason we do this is because we have not discovered that all the control actually resides within us.

This model of the world is also referred to as 'Below the Line' thinking or the lower model of the world. If there were a line drawn in the sand, each model of the world would be represented on either side of the line. Being "at Cause" keeps one below the line because we are unable to change what others are doing, thinking or how they are behaving. We are only able to change our response to them.

Being at Effect or The Emotionally Mature View of the World

Being at effect is what happens as a result of a cause. It's what happens after the cause or how one chooses to respond to the event. To determine the effect we ask the question "what happened?"

This second way of thinking is having the awareness that events, things and people do affect us and it's our internal references that create our reactions. Based on our perceptions and internal references we all respond differently to the same event. If someone makes a statement using colorful language, depending on our culture, our values and beliefs we will all respond differently.

When we are aware that we are in control of our own reactions and responses, we then make assessments about them. We are no longer blaming or laying responsibility elsewhere for how we respond. We now act from a place of choice, we can choose to be a victim of the cause or recognize that we cannot change the cause but we can change our response to any given event.

Operating from this upper model of the world allows us to take our "power" back. It puts us back into the driver's seat and creates many more possibilities for growth, awareness and change. In knowing that one has the ability to look at an event from our own internal perceptions and at the same time change how we choose to perceive this event, it opens up a world of freedom. We are no longer dependent on anything outside of ourselves for our sense of wellbeing and happiness.

There are three basic ways we react internally in this second model of the world: they are self-concept, how it feels and patterns.

We have a *"Self Concept"* which is created by our judgments, attitudes and beliefs about ourselves. It's how we see things, our view of the world and ourselves. What's right or wrong, what looks like fun or pleasure, our moral viewpoint.

Next, we have *"How it feels"*. These are the emotions that are attached to our point of view. The emotional fix we get from an object, food or event. The way we feel when we hear our favorite song, smell something delicious, or the pain that we have attached to a specific event or memory.

Then there are our *"Patterns"*. These are our habitual coping skills we use in any given circumstance. The patterns are our internal programs and the different ways we have repeatedly done things, making them an automatic way of thinking, doing and performing.

When we start to awaken and discover what we are doing internally and how we are doing it, we can then begin creating emotional control. We then have the ability to question our "self concepts", "how it feels" and our "patterns ", allowing us to make the changes necessary to respond to our world with a more evolved, mature and higher thinking process. This model of the world is often referred to as 'above the line' thinking or the upper model of the world. It's from this place that we are ready for change. We are ready to work on changing these subconscious patterns, beliefs and emotions. So how do we do that? The way to achieve changes is to use "the ART of change."

7

The ART of Change

"They say that time changes things, but you actually have to change them yourself"

~ Andy Warhol

There is an art to making the changes needed to make new imprints on the subconscious mind. Often people start with the conscious mind, making a decision that change is necessary. Whilst becoming conscious that changes need to happen is the first step on the journey, it is also where the conscious mind begins to end its usefulness in the process.

If we look at the major functions of the conscious mind we are able to understand better the need to develop a plan to bypass that critical part of the conscious mind and step into the depths of the subconscious to make our changes.

The conscious mind is known for its ability to be analytical, it allows us to analyze data coming in, make decisions about that data and solve problems. The rational part of the conscious mind takes in the events and decisions and comes up with reasons and answers for everything you do and if it doesn't get it right it will create anxious, restless symptoms until or unless it finds a reason, whether that reason makes sense or not. It's these two functions that usually trip us up when trying to instill change. With the constant analyzing and rationalizing its difficult to get past these two functions to reach the automatic processes in the subconscious that are running the beliefs that keep us trapped in our problems.

Will power is also a part of our conscious mind, and usually has very little to do with lasting change. Will power is a temporary burst of energy, that can sometime last for a while but is not sustainable in the long term. Everyone can relate to having a strong sense of will power when making a resolution… only to have the RAS (reticular activating system) pull us back to the automatic patterns of safety again. Temporary memory is another aspect of our conscious mind; it's the part of the mind that supplies bits and pieces of information that we need to get through the day. When we look at the functions of the conscious mind we can start to see why trying to instill lasting change using only this part of our mind is not very successful.

So how do we get past all of this to make permanent changes to imprints most of us can't even remember? It's all in the type of questions we ask.

ART is an acronym for Aim, Release and Transform. The huge success of Faster EFT is based on the quality of questions asked before the tapping begins and by paying close attention to the demeanor, expressions, emotions and every word uttered in response to the aiming questions.

Faster EFT has a framework for working with problems and finding the underlying issues that the conscious mind isn't able to identify. The ART of Change is a process that is all about the questions we ask before and during the tapping process. It's what leads us to the underlying issue. Often we think we know what the issue is or have an idea where are problems come from. More often than not what we think is the problem is only the tip of the iceberg. What needs to happen is we need to get to what's under the surface. In order to get to this elusive place we ask a whole set of questions that make up a powerful framework enabling you to change any issue to the outcome you desire.

Each of our problems has a unique structure:

- A belief system
- Memories and proofs to back it up.
- Many neural pathways
- Family dynamics and where we fit into the family system
- Secondary gains
- Unconscious resources

The most powerful part of Faster EFT is **aiming**. What is aiming? It is noticing how you know your problem is a problem. Direct your conscious awareness to the internal representation of a negative emotion or impression within your body and mind. We then begin to ask the aiming questions that bypass the conscious mind and direct the unconscious mind to a primary imprint.

ART of Change Questions

What you don't want

If we are to aim at the specific problem we have to get an understanding of its origins and the structure that supports it. The conscious mind is often unable to identify these things. The aiming process is crucial because it helps us bypass that critical part of our mind and it develops a map for disassembling the issue.

- *How do you know you have this problem?*

Defining exactly how we know there is a problem in the first place gives us clues to how the unconscious creates the problem. Asking how do you know it is a problem and asking where does it show up in your life? Take note of everything said after this question. This will give the blueprint for releasing and changing the issue to a positive imprint.

The next question we ask is:

- *How do you know you don't want to have this problem?*

This question allows us to see if we are really ready to

let go of our problem. Sometimes we think we are ready to let go of our issues but we have created an identity around them. Or, the problems keep us in our comfort zone and we may be unsure about moving forward. This question also helps us identify any secondary gains that we may obtain from this issue. Sometimes, we are actually gaining something from having the issue, for example, if we are seeking love and attention, our issue may be getting us attention from those we so desperately want it from. If we let it go, will they still give us the attention?

- *Have you ever experienced this before?*

This question can lead to clues of exactly what formula the mind is using to know when and how to have the problem. It is important to understanding that our fears are wishes and affirmations just as much as a positive affirmation is. We tend to spend a lot more time thinking of fearful or negative affirmations than we do on positive ones. Our personal blind spot often keeps us from consciously noticing that we are repeating patterns. Stopping and looking back to see if we have experienced something like this previously often becomes an eye opener to many patterns that have been running, but which we have been unable to consciously see.

- *Eliciting what is the worst of the worst about the problem. What is the worst of the worst about what we don't want?*

The worst of the worst about what we don't want identifies what is driving the issue. If we know what the worst of the worst is, it shows us what we have been running from, yet we have been inadvertently running towards it by continuingly rehearsing the issues. It also allows us to see that we focus on avoiding the worst of the worst which results in the worst being brought closer to reality.

- *Who else do we know that has/ had the problem or has experienced the same issue or problems and if so what happened and how long ago?*

This helps us recognize the patterns that run through our lives and whether if we are acting out someone else's issue. Have we modeled our parent's problems and taken them to be our own? Write it all down for the tapping session as it becomes the guide or map to how we have our issue.

Understanding the belief about the problem gives vital clues in how to flip the internal representation. It gives us the structure of the belief systems operating within us.

It is also what we believe is keeping us from having what we really want.

These questions give us the structure of the problem. The answers to the questions will give us enough to map out what needs to be tapped on.

What we do Want

Next, it is important to define exactly what it is that we do want. Many people are more aware of what they don't want than what exactly it is that they do want.

- *What do you want in regards to this issue?*

We need to recognize that what we say we want actually send outs warning signals to the RAS (reticular activating system). For lack of a better way of saying it, if we actually get what we want, it will upset the reticular activating system , which sends warning signals to the mind that we are off track and must get back to the norm as fast as possible. Unless those references are taken offline the RAS will keep pulling us back to the familiar (the problem).

Do we really want it? Or is it safer to say we want it as having our issue gives us a safe way out of having to step outside of our comfort zone.

We are now ready to release and transform. Allow the feeling to be fully present and intensify the feeling to an amplified state. **Releasing** is using tapping as a tool to release the negative state associated with the problem. **Transform** is when we change the problem to a positive outcome.

The next step is to start tapping. We tap on each part and piece until all emotions or internal references discovered through the questioning process are tapped down to zero. As each person taps and the memory begin to change, we tap on every new reference that comes up in between each tapping round. We are releasing the past memory and the present pain together at the same time.

Who Am I

The biggest issue that most of us face as we begin this process is "I have this problem. Who will I be if I let all of this go?" We often say that we are tired of the issues that are keeping us stuck but we have no idea just how much of our identity has been built on the very problems that we want to let go of. How often have you heard someone say: "I'm a cancer patient", "My parents had the same thing, it must be hereditary." "I'm an anxiety sufferer." "I have panic attacks," "I'm an addict or alcoholic". The truth is we are not those things. They are labels we give ourselves. We are not cancer… cancer is something we experience.

The same is true with anxiety, panic attacks or stress. Each of these things is something we do, not have. As we start to work through our issues we start to notice that the essence of whom we are changes. The releasing of the emotional charge allows for a change to happen with our perceptions.

You will know you've really healed something when you take your worst memory and make it your greatest experience. In this world of duality we often look at each experience and only view one half of the gift that the experience offers. More often than not we focus on the negative aspect but by taking the emotions offline it opens us up to see the other side of the coin and see the positive aspect of the experience.

Many years ago I suffered a traumatic experience. This experience I perceived as very negative and it shaped a large portion of my life as a victim. Several attempts at 'healing' this aspect of my life helped improve my outlook, but deep inside I still felt that this experience left me emotionally scarred and still felt like a victim of circumstance. Once I was able to tap out all the emotional charge from this experience I was asked what the gift of this experience was. I have to admit, I was stumped for a few moments. Sitting there with no emotion attached to 'the story' it became so clear... that event was the catalyst for my desire to grow and heal which then lead me to become the healer and teacher I am today.

The Future

This last part of the formula is a way of checking to see if all pathways to the problem have been addressed. It is also used as an ecology check. It is important to assess if that which we say we want in the future is in the best interest for all concerned. It is important to make sure that what someone is moving toward is going to be in their best interest or whether anyone else that might also be affected by the outcome. This is also known as future pacing. We use our imagination to go forward into the future to see how we would respond to the same issues that in the past had bothered us. Keeping in mind that the unconscious is unable to tell the difference between what is real and what is imagined, this gives a good indication of what has been cleared and what hasn't. Future pacing is also useful to create outcomes that are desirable in much the same way that we currently produce the problems we have. By using the unconscious mind and feelings to project and move toward a desired outcome, we start to develop new pathways to the brain that brings the desired outcome into our reality quicker.

Whether we are working with someone or working on ourselves, paying close attention to the physical and emotional responses lets us know if there is more work to be done. When we are working with someone it is important to notice the facial expressions as you ask a person to imagine a future date and then have the same issue arise. If you are paying close attention, you will notice small shifts in a persons face if they are not congruent with the changes that have been made, such as a slight twitching of the eyes; lips may lose color and other involuntary movements. If any of these arise it is always good practice to go back and clean up anything that might be left. At this point it is also beneficial to picture the people involved with our issue and look them in the eyes. Often this will reveal any unresolved emotions or references that might have otherwise gone unnoticed. If we find that there are still triggers we then go back to tapping until all references are gone and the internal representation has been flipped to a positive one. Also, looking forward with a positive reference starts to lay the foundation for the new neural pathways to a more positive outcome.

Future pacing can also be used in laying the foundation for what types of outcomes and responses we would like to have to any number of events. It can be used in goal setting and checking out how the body responds to the goal we are setting.

8

Memories and the Trance State

"Because we already live with many scripts that have been handed down to us, the process of writing our own script is actually more a process of 'rescripting', or paradigm shifting - of changing some of the basic paradigms we already have."

~Stephen Covey

What is Real?

Faster EFT operates within a framework that states 'the present moment' is the only moment that is real. It is the only time that one has active choices; everything else is a memory or a trance state. What this means is, the present moment is the only moment in consciousness that we can actually make any choice in, change in any way.

When we are not conscious in the moment we are either retrieving past information stored in our mind by neural clusters or we are imagining what could be possible in the future. Anytime we take our awareness away from the present moment we enter a "trance" state. It is **the present moment** that we are fully aware and conscious of, yet many of us miss the present moment by spending much of our time and awareness either in what happened in the past or what might happen in the future.

Take a moment and ask yourself, how present am I? Are you here, fully present reading the words on this page or even as you are reading this are you asking yourself what needs to happen to get ready for what lies ahead or are you remembering something that was said on this very topic previously and if so, recognize that you have drifted off and spent a moment in the past.

The Past is over and does not Exist

Most of us think of our negative beliefs as if the people involved are actually people in our head trying to make our life miserable! It is a bit like thinking that every file in our documents folder is actually a real piece of paper; they do not become real until we "print" them out. So where is everything in the computer stored? Just like in our unconscious mind, the beliefs and memories are patterns of energy that are stored via energy being held in an electromagnetic field. When we disrupt that field with a virus or a new program; the pattern changes. Just like changing or deleting files on the computer, the memories or beliefs we hold in our memory can be altered or deleted just as quickly.

Memories are not real, yet they feel real because we feel them physically. The past is over and does not exist; once the moment has passed we can never reclaim it or change what actually transpired. In order to recall a "memory" we have to go through a thought process and take our awareness away from the present moment. This sets off the chain reaction in the mind that uses our meridian system to send signals to our physical body to produce a feeling.

When we are unaware of our present moment we have entered a "trance". Hypnosis or "trance" is our minds ability to imagine, feel & follow what we imagine as if it's real. A "trance" is our automated programs that have been operating for years.

Take a moment, close your eyes and remember the first time you were kissed. In your mind's eye, see what you saw, hear what you heard and feel what you felt during that first kiss. Where were you, who else was there, did you enjoy it? Now open your eyes, did you notice that by thinking about that first kiss, you had a memory come up? Did you feel what you had felt back then, yet, here you are. It's not actually happening but your body had a response to the memory or thought around it.

Maybe you noticed that it brought back certain feelings, or a sense of smell of where you were when it happened.

9

Why Do We Tap

"Tapping is a lot like toilet paper. It only works if you use it. If you don't use it, you have a rash of stinky problems."
~Robert G. Smith

The overall goal of **FasterEFT** is to **Change the Structure** of our memories. Our memories are made up of many smaller pieces. In changing the interpretation of what those pieces mean and by changing the memory and clearing the emotional charge the memory had, then we can remove the problem. Memories are a reflection of our internal belief structures expressed as a metaphor that represents who and how we are in the world.

If the memories are not real, if they are just internal representations or stories, then why do we need to change them? We need to go back to the primitive brain or amygdala, the filing cabinet of all our experiences. We tap in order to change how things are stored in the amygdala, the part of the brain that creates the fight or flight response.

During the experience of a negative feeling or emotion, by tapping on the meridian points, the body sends back to the brain the message that everything is okay in the physical system, allowing the primitive part of the brain to turn off the "Danger" signals. The filing cabinet then replaces the old memory with the new emotional response. By eliciting the problem or negative emotion, we then immediately tap till the emotion is gone. In this way we then create a new, more positive emotion and it collapses the problem all together. We can create a whole new "US" by changing how we hold ourselves inside our mind.

Faster EFT uses meridian points and tapping which is a process founded in Acupressure. Acupressure is an ancient healing art that uses the fingers to press key points on the surface of the skin to stimulate the body's natural self-curative abilities. When the points are pressed, they release muscle tension and promote the circulation of blood and the body's life force that aids in healing. Acupuncture and acupressure both use the same points, but acupuncture employs needles, while acupressure uses the gentle but firm pressure of hands/fingers or touch. Acupressure was neglected after the Chinese developed more technology driven methods for stimulating points with needles and electricity.

How Acupressure Works

Acupressure points are places on the skin that are especially sensitive to bioelectrical impulses in the body. These points conduct those impulses readily. Stimulating these points with pressure, needles, or heat, triggers the release of endorphins which are the neuro-chemicals that relieve pain. As a result, pain is blocked and the flow of blood and oxygen to the affected area is increased. This causes the muscles to relax and promotes healing.

Because acupressure inhibits the pain signals sent to the brain through a mild and painless stimulation, it has been described as shutting the "doors" of the pain-signaling system, preventing painful sensations from passing through the spinal cord to the brain. In addition to relieving pain, acupressure can help rebalance the body by dissolving tensions and stresses that keep it from functioning smoothly and which inhibit the immune system.

Tension tends to concentrate around acupressure points. When a muscle is chronically tense or in spasm, the muscle fibers contract due to the secretion of lactic acid caused by fatigue, trauma, stress, chemical imbalances or poor circulation. By pressing the pressure point, the tension in the muscle yields to the finger pressure, stimulating and enabling the fibers to elongate and relax. The blood starts to flow freely and the toxins are released and eliminated. As the circulation is increased it brings more oxygen and other nutrients to those affected areas. When the bioelectrical energy and the blood circulate properly, it creates a greater sense of harmony, well-being and health.

The healing benefits of acupressure involve both the relaxation of the body and its positive effects on the mind. As tension is released, you not only feel good physically, but you also feel better emotionally and mentally. When our body relaxes, our mind relaxes as well, creating another state of consciousness. This expanded awareness leads to mental clarity and a healthier physical and emotional healing dissolving the division between the mind and body.

The meridian points used in Faster EFT represent our organs. The organs produce chemicals and electrical impulses that create the 'fight or flight' response. Stress and emotion are the expressions of perceived threats.

Tapping on the meridian points disrupts the electrical/chemical system, it breaks the emotional connection by working within the mind/body system. Tapping creates a roadblock in the mind/body pathway, disrupting that electrical/chemical system and sending a different message back to the mind allowing the perception to shift, thus giving you control over your unconscious resources, and pulling you into the present moment.

When we tap with Faster EFT it is the original memory or primary imprint that we are aiming to release the emotional charge around. The primary imprint has the emotional combination of the how to, what to do, the driving force to act. This is based on what has been internalized from a previous specific event or from combined experiences using one main reference point.

The primary principle is a belief system that is created from an imprinted experience or experiences that are stacked up, stored and we refer to or automatically kick in stay in until we find a better way or we re-write the primary imprints then create a new imprint to operate from.

Example:

"I hate crowded places."

How do you know?

"When I was a little girl I got lost in the Shopping Centre, and couldn't find my mother. There were too many people and I couldn't find her, I was so scared I got sick in the stomach. I thought something bad would happen to me."

The imprinted experience is what creates the behavior. Even though the getting sick was not caused by all the people in the Shopping Centre, but by not being able to find her mother and her level of fear, what the child perceived was that there were too many people there and that's what made her get lost and get sick. So crowds will trigger an emotional response based on the imprinted experience.

Flipping a memory is a re-patterning, re- imprinting or re-representing of a memory. We change how we hold the memory completely, changing or "flipping it" so a positive outcome is represented and re-imprinted in our minds. Keeping in mind that the memory is no longer real, it is only a representation of the mind and the purpose of "flipping it" is to create a healthier, more positive imprint.

10

How to Tap Faster EFT Style

"Tap until it's gone or until you pass out. Either way you will wake up to a whole new day."
~ Robert G. Smith

So, you're ready to start tapping and let go of all those issues and memories that have kept you stuck for so long. Where do you begin and how do you actually tap? Well, with Faster EFT the first thing you do is to write your "Peace List". We want to pull the whole emotional tree out, roots and all. The "peace list" represents the tree and its roots; we need to list everything that could be supporting the issues or problems. We list everything because consciously we don't know what is supporting the problems, or the associations that the subconscious mind has made to different events and listing everything will enable us to get to the root of the problem. The list gives us a place to start changing the primary imprints.

The Peace List

The Peace List is a list that is compiled in bullet-point form of all the memories, issues, events, resentments, fears, traumas, moves, schools, job losses, all your relationships, any physical, emotional or pivotal points and anything else that comes to mind. List any experiences you remember from your childhood, list 'suspected' experiences you have no real memory about. This list is usually easier to compile than a list of things you would like to feel peaceful about.

Understanding the power of what you don't want will give you a better understanding of what makes the "Peace List" so important. Many people come to me and say that they've had enough; they are sick and tired of all the rubbish in their lives. When asked about ***what they do want***, most people are stumped. We then begin talking again about what it is that we don't want. The problem with this is because the focus remains on what we don't want, it gives incredible power to the very things that we say we don't want. We move on to become experts at producing the very thing we don't want and spend our lives in the never-ending loop of ***talking about and producing*** just that, ***what we don't want.***

If you remember the RAS (reticular activating system) we spoke of earlier, you'll see why continuing to repeat what you don't want is not a good strategy. The RAS receives over two billion sensory inputs a minute. The purpose of our RAS system is to filter out what is not important to us and bring into focus what is important to us. Just like an antenna, continuing to repeat what you don't want sets the controls of the antenna up to search that out and bring it into your field of awareness. Your attention is drawn to what you believe to be true… and it works the same whether you focus on what you want or if you focus on what you don't want. When there is a lot of energy invested in focusing on what you don't want you begin to see, feel or hear that everywhere. So why do we start with what we don't want?

Starting with a peace list also allows us to have a starting place for tapping. If you already have a few issues that you know you want to work on, great… it is suggested that you still go ahead and write out a peace list so that when the big issues have been cleared, you still have a direction to be moving in. We all will be clearing past representations for the rest of our lives.

Measuring Stress Levels

You will need a way to measure the levels of progress as well as the levels of stress that may still be present after each round of tapping in order to tell if the stress is actually decreasing. For this we will be using Subject Units of Distress. The Subjective Units of Distress Scale (SUD), originally developed by Wolpe (1969) provides a precise way to measure change in a client's self-reported emotional state. It is a widely accepted psychological tool of measurement and can be used for almost any kind of problem as a way of quantifying the intensity of your feelings, emotions, pain or stress. Here is how that works:

> First you will bring to mind a memory or issue. Take notice of how you know you are feeling it. Is it a mental picture, something you feel, or something you remember hearing? Notice, how you know, then gauge the intensity of it on a scale of 0 to 10;

- 0 is the bottom end of the scale – there are no emotions or symptoms present and you feel calm and relaxed.

- 5 is the middle of the scale – you are feeling some discomfort, but you are able to stand it.

- 8 is where the level of discomfort is severe.

- 10 is being as upset as you were during the initial event and the discomfort is as intense as it can get. 0 being no feeling or reaction to the memory or event at all.

Write this rating down or just take a mental note of where you are on this scale in regards to the issue being worked on.

The next step will be to be 'amp up' that level of distress, really allow yourself to feel what was happening. The purpose of this is to intensify the feelings in order to clarify how much distress it represents in your life. Amplifying it allows you to focus on and aim at those feelings that need to be released.

Always measure the level of intensity as it exists for you right now in the present moment, not how you would think it would be in the actual situation. After a round of tapping, when you check in with how you're feeling, you might have shifted the intensity to a lower number but it is not completely gone. This is an indication that the issue is not completely resolved and that more rounds of tapping are required, persisting until the intensity is down to a 0 is the goal.

The real value of using this model is to get insight into how you currently view the problem – your model of the world and your reference system. You are breaking down how you've created the problem in your own mind.

What is interesting is the phenomenon that happens around the physical discomfort, or symptoms when tapping. You may find that they sometimes change in nature or move to a different part of the body. For example, if you are working with an emotion, you might notice that the emotion you started with disappears and that a different one takes its place or a headache might turn into an ache somewhere else in the body, or disappear all together only for you to notice that you are now instead feeling tension in your shoulders. This is very common when tapping; often there are underlying emotions that sit just under the surface of the emotion that we think we are feeling. When this happens continue tapping but focus on the current emotion, feeling, picture, or statement that comes up.

Set up Phrase

Faster EFT uses a 'set up' phrase that is entirely different from the one used in traditional EFT. The set up phrase is used to set the stage for our unconscious mind, to go ahead and let go of whatever issue we are working on. Our minds have become so good at avoiding or 'staying safe' that using only our conscious mind to work on our issue slows the process down incredibly. In order to be able to work directly with the unconscious, the place that all our automated responses originate, we need to use a set up phrase to bypass the conscious mind and work directly with the unconscious. This is not complicated and can be done with the following phrases:

> Once the feelings or memories have been intensified, ask;

> *"If I were holding a bunch of helium balloons in my hand and I opened my hand, what would naturally happen?"*

> Or *"If I were to dig up a tree by the roots, what would*

naturally happen to the tree?"

In both cases the person being tapped on naturally responds, "the balloons would float away" or "the tree would fall over and die." If the person doesn't respond straight away, prompt them with the answer.

The intent of the set up phrase is two fold, to pull the person out of the 'trance' or 'memory' and to bypass the conscious mind, giving the subconscious permission to let go of what ever is being tapped on. These set up phrases are metaphors for the unconscious to let go or release the dominant feeling, memory or issue. You can use the metaphors here or choose another metaphor that represents letting go and doesn't need a lot of explanation.

The FASTER EFT Tapping Points

Faster EFT uses the primary meridian for disrupting emotional triggers:

- *Between the eyes or Eyebrow point* – (Bladder) this tapping point starts at the beginning of the eyebrow, just above and to one side of the nose.

- ***Temples or the side of the eyes*** – (Gallbladder) This point is on the bone bordering the outside corner of the eye.

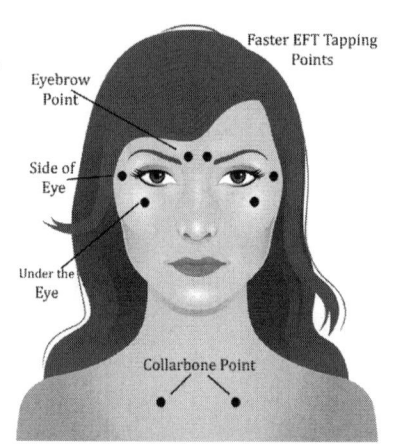

- ***Under the eyes*** – (Stomach) Tap on the bone under the eye in the center of the cheek.

- ***Collar bone*** – (Kidney) put your fingers in the hollow of your throat and feel for the two heads of the collarbones on either side, then tap directly underneath the collarbone.

Wrist – (lungs, large intestine, circulation, heart, & triple warmer) take either hand, wrap your hand around the other wrist and give it a gentle squeeze.

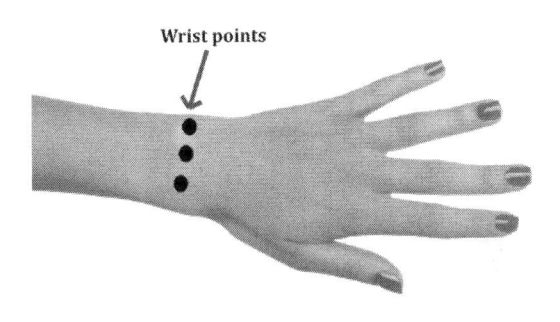

Wrist points

When tapping it doesn't matter if you are left handed or right handed or want to use both hands to tap. The meridian points used in Faster EFT hit all the organs responsible for the creation of the fight and flight response.

You might notice that there are fewer tapping points than in traditional EFT, while this is true the Faster EFT tapping points operate just as effectively. In working with thousands of people, Robert Smith found that it was not necessary to use all the tapping points to affect change. By using the tapping points in FasterEFT change happens in a faster, more expedient way.

Aim & Tap

What is aiming? Aiming is one of the most powerful aspects of the Faster EFT process. When we aim we ask whoever is being tapped on to "notice how you know", bringing conscious awareness to an internal representation of a negative emotion or impression within your body and mind. As we tap the negative state moves toward zero and then crosses over into a positive expression.

1. Ask, "How do you know?" Is it an image, sound, feeling?
2. Notice how you know and where you feel it in your body.
3. Identify it and notice how you know it.
4. When you start to tap, tap on the Faster EFT points in the diagram and focus on and feel where the fingers are actually tapping. Say and repeat "I release and let go of this _____, as you move to each meridian point, repeat; "I let it go, let it go, let it go, it is safe to let it go."
5. Take a deep breath, blow it out and say "Peace".

6. Ask, "How has it changed?" aim at it again, notice what's left, then go back to it and tap it out with the same tapping points.
7. If you find that emotions are starting to bubble up as you tap, bring your attention to the overwhelming feelings and then notice and bring your attention to the actual tapping. Then go back to noticing the feelings and back to the feeling of the tapping on your skin. Go in and out of the feelings.
8. Don't stop tapping until all the emotion is gone or the intensity has dropped down to a zero SUDS rating.
9. "Flip the memory", change the internal representation of the memory, re-patterning, or re-imprinting. We 'flip it' so that a positive outcome occurs and is re-imprinted in our minds.

The TOTEMS Model

The T.O.T.E concept maintains that all mental and behavioral programs revolve around having a fixed goal and a variable means to achieve that goal. It indicates that, as we think, we set goals in our mind both consciously and unconsciously and then we develop a TEST for when that goal has been achieved. If it's not achieved, we then OPERATE to change something or do something to get us closer to our goal. When the TEST criteria have been satisfied, we EXIT.

When this model of addressing problems is used you create powerful results. When you have reached a SUDS rating of zero you know you are done. We then go out and test the results in real life, checking or testing (operating) to make sure it's all gone.

Faster EFT adds two more processes to the T.O.T.E model, these are M-make it come back in the same or any other way and S-switch it, or flip it so the person is re-imprinted with a positive memory. These last two steps allow us to make sure that we have completely taken the problem offline and switched how it is being represented in the unconscious mind.

T – Test- Check the problem or issue and give it a 0-10 rating.

O – Operate - Address the problem by tapping or other techniques

T – Test – Check it again by using the 0-10 SUDS rating and if not 0 continue tapping until it is 0.

E – Exit – When you test and there is no emotion left then exit.

M – Make it come back - Have the person being tapped on try and make the feeling come back.

S – Switch it or Flip it - Flip the internal representation and re-imprint with a positive memory.

11

Faster EFT Tapping Techniques

"Happiness is the result of who you are inside and how you view the world."

Robert G. Smith

There are several different tapping processes used in Faster EFT. The first process is a very simple easy to use process and works wonders on just about any issue.

The Quick Tap

First, you will need to decide what problem or issue you want to address. Notice how it is a problem or issue. In other words, define the issue and or notice how you know it is a problem. For example, let's say you are worried about your performance at work. You'll discover when asking yourself "How do I know I'm worried about my performance?" that you will start to experience physical symptoms such as your heart starting to beat faster or a knot in your stomach or emotions may start to surface, like irritation, or anger when you think that someone may be judging your performance.

1. Recall the event, issue or problem in detail. (Notice the emotions and or specific things that support the problem, i.e. physical symptoms).

2. Close your eyes and really allow yourself to associate with the issue or problem bearing in mind "The stronger you feel it, the faster it will go".

3. Tell yourself to go there and feel it for the last time.

4. Give the feelings, picture or issue a SUDS rating then amp it up.

5. Open your eyes and for a moment imagine a tree in front of you. Imagine if you were to pull the roots out from under the tree, what would naturally happen to a tree without roots? That's right, it would naturally fall over and die.

6. Close your eyes again and start tapping, bring your attention to the way your fingers feel on

your skin as you tap and say the following out loud:

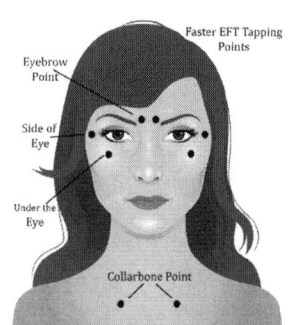

- Tap on the eyebrow point: "I am releasing and letting go of all:
- All sadness's, all fears, all emotional traumas,
- Side of the eye: all the angers, resentments, guilt's,
- Under the eye: All the judgments, abandonments, all betrayals,
- Collarbone: All the helplessness, hopelessness, feelings of no control, rejections and everything else".
- Grab the wrist, squeeze lightly and say "That's right, let it all go, It's safe to let this go".
- Take a deep breath, blow it out and say "Peace".

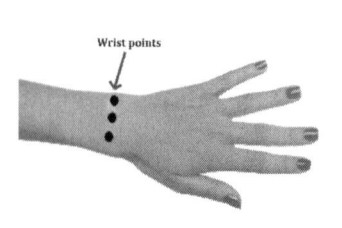

- Recheck the problem and notice how it has changed. Look for any other emotion or physical reaction that may have come up.
- Notice what has changed and how it has changed. E.g.; has the pressure changed, has the feeling lessened or increased, has the pain decreased, moved or developed elsewhere.
- Notice what is left of the issue, emotion, or physical feeling.
- Go back in by closing your eyes and start the tapping sequence again, all the while saying "That's right let it go, let it go, it's safe to let this go, I let it all go now". Take a deep breath, blow it out and say "Peace".
- Using the T.O.T.E.M.S model keep repeating the last sequence until you can no longer make it come back at all, in any way, shape or form.
- Switch the internal representation; what was the true gift of the experience. Replace the negative reference with a positive reference. For example, how would you have liked for the event to have happened.
- Then take a moment and place yourself in the future one month from today. If the same issue were to arise, how does it feel? Then

> forward to six months from now, see how you are feeling now that this issue is no longer affecting your life… how are you? How do you feel? What are you seeing? Now, see yourself one year, two years down the track, how are you now? What has changed in your life and how is it better? What are you doing now that you never thought you would be doing or never believed you could do? What about this issue, is it anywhere around or affecting you? Now step ahead to 5 years from now, ….

There are many other emotions that you may want to add to the tapping routine. Add whatever is the most predominant emotion showing up: Anxiety, betrayals, apathy, despair, disappointment, rage, shame, terror, frustration, hatred, terror.

Tap until there is nothing left… follow the trail of what rises up in between tapping rounds. If the picture or feeling changes, follow that, tap until all that's left is that feeling of being okay.

- **A note** about the process of taking a deep breath, blowing it away and saying "Peace". Often when we experience stress the first thing we do is hold our breath. This step encourages us to breathe while at the same time letting our unconscious mind know that we are "Blowing away" whatever stress is left.

When you get to the "Peace", take a moment and imagine a time when you felt most peaceful or recall a happy moment. Really allow yourself to go there, see what you saw, feel what you felt and hear what you were hearing when you felt the peaceful feeling. This step is important because we want to anchor in that peaceful feeling between rounds.

The Mental Tap

Mental tapping is mentally focusing on the tapping points as if you were physically tapping. It is often more powerful than physical tapping because of the amount of focus you use when tapping this way. In your mind, it's as if you are tapping all the points simply by bringing your focus to those areas as you tell yourself to "let it go".

To learn this technique, you can program yourself by physically tapping each point and then memorizing what it feels like, then follow with mentally tapping to get it set in your mind.

So, start by physically tapping, notice what it feels like, then mentally tap. Once you feel you are able to focus and recreate the tapping feeling mentally, move to the next point, continue this until you have completed the whole round. Take a deep breath, blow it away and say "Peace".

Practice until it is set in your mind how to do it then all you need to do is mentally tap each point, while silently saying "Let it go, let it go" inside yourself and when you've done all the tapping points in your minds eye, grab your wrist, take a deep breath, blow it away and say "Peace" to yourself.

1. When you notice your stress levels starting to rise, or having been triggered, imagine yourself tapping on each of the points. Silently say the words "Let it go, it's safe to let this go, I let this go now". Remembering the focus is switched to the points where you are tapping.

2. Check to see if the issue is resolved or you are feeling a peace with whatever started the stress. If not, continue to "mentally tap" until the stress level reaches a Zero on the SUDS scale.

3. Make sure that once it has reached a Zero level that you flip the memory or issue finding the gift from the specific issue or that you've reached a sense of resolution.

Expressions Technique

The benefit of using Faster EFT is that we are clearing all angles of the memories that have been plaguing us. The goal is to do that with every aspect and character in the memory. The expression technique is a way of subtly flipping memories while actually tapping on the expression on the faces of the characters in the memory.

Since Faster EFT operates from the belief that the only thing that is real is the present moment, we are aware that the characters in our memories are really aspects of ourselves, that show up for healing. With this technique we are actually rewriting how we represent ourselves by addressing the expressions on everyone involved within the memory.

1. Tap on an issue or problem as stated in earlier techniques, bringing the SUDS rating down to a Zero rating.

2. Ask yourself or the person you are tapping to describe the expression on the face of anyone else that has shown up in the memory.

3. Notice the feelings and the expression of the character that is revealed and start another round of tapping with the focus on the expression.

4. Continue to tap on the expression until it changes to something positive.

5. Apply this to every character that is in the memory.

6. Be aware that if the face disappears, it is the mind's way of avoiding that feeling, so go ahead and tap on "It's safe to see what I cannot see".

7. Continue tapping using the TOTEMS until all aspects of the memory are positive.

The Expression Technique is a valuable technique to use when someone says that they have already dealt with a memory or issue. It gives you the means to test to see if the issue or memory has really changed or flipped.

Physical Pain Technique

A powerful way to let go of any physical pain is to bring your focus to the area, identify exactly how it feels, what it represents and be willing to release it. This technique will often be the beginning point for dealing with other issues that the pain is representing. Often when I am working with physical pain I use a companion book that refers to the emotional aspects that the pain may be representing. It's like becoming a detective; our body does not lie to us and is often working hard to notify us when we are out of balance. Pain is the warning system that the physical body is trying to get our attention.

1. Identify the pain and its location.

2. Use the SUDS scale to rate the pain level on a scale of 0 to 10 with 10 being the worst pain.

3. Gather information about the aspects of the pain; how it feels, sensations, sharp, dull, pressure, constant, or pulsating, etc.

4. Ask, "If this pain had words, what would it say?" Take note of the first thing that comes to mind... this is often a map to what the issue underneath the pain is.

5. Say the 'Tree or Balloon' metaphor to yourself or whomever you are tapping. "*Imagine a tree in front of you, imagine if you were to pull the roots out from under the tree, what would naturally happen to the tree? It would fall over and die, wouldn't it.*" Or "*Imagine if I had a fist of Helium balloons in my hand, what would happen naturally if I opened my hand? The balloon would float away, wouldn't they?*"

6. Tap the Faster EFT Tapping points:

    - Between the eyebrows..."I release and let it go, I let it go..."
    - Side of the eye... "Whatever this pain represents, wherever it came from..."
    - Under the eye... "Whatever it means, it is safe to let it go..."

- Collarbone… "I choose to let it go, I let it go now."
- Grab your wrist, squeeze, take a deep breath, and blow it away and say "Peace".

7. Check the pain level; notice what is left, how has it shifted? Describe how it has changed and what aspects are left.

8. Repeat the first 7 Steps till the SUDS rating is at Zero. Be aware that the pain often shifts from one location to another. Keep tapping until all pain is gone.

9. Find the gift… or flip the memory, issue or association; this is a key part to taking the issue offline altogether.

Changing the memory is about changing how you represent the memory in your own mind, how you would like to have it represented when that filing cabinet of the mind brings it to the surface again.

For example: Getting rejected or dumped can be flipped to seeing how the relationship was not serving either party and that you have become a stronger person because you are no longer in the relationship. It is not about denying what happened, just finding the gift in it.

12

Case Studies

Case Study I

For many years I have been on a quest to find ways to overcome and undo many of my childhood traumas as well as helpless and stuck feelings. In my late twenties I found Hatha Yoga, which helped me on the road to health and wellbeing and I loved it so much I studied for three years under Swami Satchidanada for my British Wheel of Yoga teaching Diploma. I also gained a certificate in remedial and therapeutic massage, healing with herbs and looked into anything that would help me... Many years later a friend introduced me to FasterEFT while I was having difficulties and I just couldn't get a handle on my life and everything seemed to be going wrong...

Faster Emotionally Focused Transformations helped me in so many ways and on so many levels... Each time I have worked with a fellow practitioner I have had major shifts from being stuck in a job which was no longer working for me to overcoming major trauma from my childhood, to relieving menopause symptoms, I wanted to know more so I studied directly under Robert Smith and have gained my levels one, two and three certificates…

During the level three training FasterEFT training course I volunteered for a session to be tapped on about grief and loss…

So there I was, wondering how relevant the story I was about to disclose was to the subject of grief and loss… I started telling my story of how I was at my father's funeral and I was not included or even mentioned during the eulogy, which added to the already sad day and it really bothered me. On the day I remember at one point I wanted to physically stand up and say out loud, "Hello my name is Kim Masters and I'm Jim's daughter", but I didn't, I just sat there feeling really sad and rejected. I remember walking around my father's coffin and saying my goodbyes and seeing my brother in the distance standing with my father's wife and I was unable to speak with them, I just burst into tears and ran out of the building feeling so hurt by the whole ordeal and I so wanted to let go of all of that and we tapped on all the hurts and rejections…

During my session the direction changed and we went back in time to when I was a little girl and it was when

I was being sexually abused by my father. Now what I must say at this point is that I had done a lot of work around this subject and I had forgiven my father and there was no emotional charge as I saw myself in that situation again... But then I was asked where was I before I was in that situation and it was in the middle of the night and I was in bed asleep. I was then taken back to being in bed and my father was coming into my bedroom to get me and then I was asked why I didn't just scream out for help, well I found I just couldn't do it, because I was holding on to the 'BIG SECRET'. We tapped on the secret and released the secret and I was asked again to scream out for help and this time I was very aware that I may burst everyone's eardrums in the room because I was wearing a microphone, so I was told to place my hand in front of it and then attempted the scream out but this time it was a little weedy sound. More tapping around the fear and then I was asked who I wanted to scream out for and then I screamed an almighty scream "HELP MUM!" This was the flip which helped me to overcome the fears I have held all my life about standing up and speaking up for myself. Before this session I had a real fear of public speaking but the weirdest thing of all is that I have been a singer and have performed in front of thousands of people throughout my adult life but I couldn't stand up and talk and address a small group of people without stuttering or tripping over my words... (Now ever since I had my first session of FasterEFT, before I even knew what FasterEFT was, I've been literally singing the praises of this most excellent technique, I started writing songs and posting YouTube film clips). Back to the session, we were back at the funeral and I was asked to stand up and walk to the front of the funeral congregation and start singing one of my FasterEFT songs to them, well I can tell you I burst out laughing and now every time I think of my father's funeral it brings a smile to my face...

Ever since I had that amazing session my whole world has changed, because now I'm making videos, running my own talks, workshops and working with other practitioners in my community and fearlessly sharing my knowledge and wisdom about the wonderful modality and other skills I know and love with great passion and joy...

Kim Masters – Holistic Health Care Practitioner, renowned inspirational speaker and life skills coach...

Case Study II

I was thrilled to be learning this new technique... especially when it was announced that Robert Smith was doing private sessions and I was gently pushed by my friend Debra to book a session. I had never been able to get up in front a lot of people and expose my issues, so it looked like there might be hope of clearing some of my stuff since during the training everything was being filmed. After years of working on myself, moving beyond my drug and alcohol issues, yet still feeling stuck, blocked and unable to move on in a couple of areas of my life, I decided to go ahead and have a private session with the creator of this technique.

I was told to write out a list in dot point form of any and all incidents, events, resentments, moves, or anything that I felt might need to be cleared. My first thought was "You are kidding right?" The session was only going to be two hours, a list like that would surely take the better part of a whole day of work wouldn't it?.

I completed my list and headed for my appointment. The closer I got my anxiety levels rose drastically… I couldn't understand it. I almost decided to pull out of the session, yet another part of me was determined to see if this would work where so many other things I had tried had helped but not cleared my issues.

The session went quickly, nothing seemed to stand out… the only issue that seemed to be highlighted was a sexual abuse issue… I had blocked it for many years and had only become aware of it in my thirties. After the emotions had been tapped down to zero… and the expression technique was used, I was asked to describe what the gift of this experience was… completely taken aback, I responded that I wasn't sure that there was any. I was told that there are always gifts, we usually only focus on the negative gift, so what was the positive gift from this experience? It took me a couple of minutes, but then it hit me, my whole adult life has been dedicated to helping others, especially people that suffer from addictions. If this particular event hadn't happened I probably would not have spent the better half of my life working on myself and then teaching others what I have learnt. At that moment, I felt the flip happen in my physical body. The session continued and we got through the rest of my very exhaustive list. I left that session honestly thinking, "What's the big deal? I could have done that at home". And it's true, I probably could have, but I wouldn't have found the gift or been able to flip how I represented that particular event in my mind.

Two months later, someone pointed out that I had toenails... who cares, right? Well, I have never, ever had toenails... I mean never, my whole life.... I would rip them off, tear at them, and nothing I had tried in the past to stop this behavior worked. But sure enough, I needed a pedicure!

So, you say, not that big a deal, right? Well, then I had the opportunity to go and spend some time with family members... not just a short amount of time, but an extended amount of time. What happened next just blew my mind. I spent that trip with family and not once did I get triggered. Not an argument, not a melt down, not even a single misunderstanding. In all my life I have never been able to spend more than a few days around my family; I would get so triggered and fall into the helpless, hopeless victim, this was an absolute first. It was so healing not just for me, but also for everyone involved. Never in my wildest dreams did I think I would be able to move past this experience. My whole life it had haunted me and now it's just a story.

Kim Jewell... Advanced Level IV Faster EFT Practitioner, Author, Renowned Inspirational Teacher and Speaker.

Case Study III

On a recent trip to Sydney, I was staying with friends and had been asked by my friend Sally to give her advice on a problem she was having at work. After listening to what she described as her problem I suggested that we do some Faster EFT. My friend was convinced it wasn't her that was the problem but a co-worker. Here is what she had to say after tapping.

I have had a few sessions with Kim, but I have had the most extraordinary week after she last tapped on me a week ago. Somebody I work with, from the day they started, has caused me a great deal of angst and resentment. After my session with Kim last weekend, I went to work on Monday feeling fabulous and was told by a co-worker I was much chirpier than usual. The extraordinary part was I no longer had these feelings toward this person – I mean really! Without any particular effort, I found I was able to speak with her at ease and by the end of the week was genuinely interested in what she had to say. From thinking about resigning because of this person, to having such a completely different perspective, if it hadn't happened to me, I might not have believed it. The focus of my session with Kim had not even been on this person, but the amazing way she has of getting to what is really going on with you and helping you to let it all go is the key to a happier, more at peace self.

Moral of my story? Keep tap tap tapping.

Sally –Sydney

Case Study IV

As a client I often don't feel that there is an issue to work on when attending a session. On this particular occasion this was indeed the case, so I opted to tap on my inability to move past a financial ceiling that had seemed to prevent me from moving forward in my business. This seemed simple and vague enough, I thought I would be safe from having to experience any uncomfortable feelings.

As the session began and we started tapping, I got this image of my Father sitting at the kitchen table smoking a cigarette. I really didn't think it had anything to do with the subject or myself, so I didn't say anything. As my practitioner, Vee Evans started to tap again, I got this overwhelming, annoying feeling that she wasn't tapping hard enough, which seemed oddly coincidental, because with the image of my father, he was telling me that it was a hard life out there and I would never make it in the big, bad world. So, I told the practitioner, and she thought it was important and we followed that line of tapping.

The next thing I knew the image had shifted and it was now an image of my father again, sitting at the dinner table just before he passed away. In this image, as it had happened, I had looked up from my dinner and knew he was dying. I quickly looked back down at my food and tried to tell myself it was my imagination. He passed away within the hour of a pulmonary embolism.

In the session, as that image appeared, a domino effect happened. I had been told by my father at age 17 to either go to a 12- step meeting or move out. I had opted for the latter. On that fateful day that my father passed, I had returned home for three days to visit and had not had a drink for a week. My father had said hours earlier that he was a big man and could admit it when he was wrong. He had bought a bottle of whiskey and we were to have a drink when dinner was finished. Only dinner didn't get to finish, he had gotten up from the table abruptly and left to go to the hospital... I never saw him again.

While we were tapping on that image of him at the table and me looking up, knowing he was dying, I got it - I had hid, looked away and tried to pretend it wasn't real. It had been my chance to tell him that he had been right all along, but I wanted the drink more. The realization hit me so hard, I tried to speak, but my throat had closed, the practitioner kept tapping. I also saw in that moment that I had been living a legacy... he had been right about the drinking, he must be right about me not being able to make it in the big, bad, world out there. So... in honor of him, every time I got close to reaching a level of success I would retreat and make up reasons why I wasn't ready, or the timing wasn't right.

It is important to note that the drinking had not been an issue in my life anymore, I had stopped drinking two years after my father passed, yet I was still hitting a glass ceiling with my success. The other interesting thing that the session showed me was since I had put the alcohol and drugs down, I had this unbelievable need to be honest, authentic and congruent in everything I did. In that instant, while the dominoes were falling, I saw why that had happened, I had had my chance to tell him the truth but just couldn't in that moment. While tapping I was able to forgive myself, flip how I held the memory of that moment, thank my father for being one of my greatest teachers and see how he had been instrumental in turning my life around. The new perception became one of him supporting me while I continue to help others uncover and discover their true potential.

Two days later, I felt the overwhelming urge to write this book and share with the world, something so simple, easy and one of the greatest gifts in my life.

Happy tapping…

About the Author:

Kim Jewell lives in Brisbane Australia where she has a private practice and specializes in helping others in their struggle with addiction.

Kim's personal journey is one of courage and success, recovery from addiction, alcoholism, anxiety and more. This journey allows her to combine her education and experience working with clients with the newly evolving field of energy psychology.

Drawing on her many life experiences, talents and expertise, Kim blends principles from NLP, Faster EFT, The Journey, The Law of Attraction, Present Moment Awareness, Energy Psychology, Reiki and more, to facilitate the uncovering and discovery of ones highest potential.

Kim has written *From Stress to Success, Faster Emotionally Focused Transformations* after experiencing first hand the profound effects Faster EFT had on her own personal transformation and out of the desire to share with the world a healing modality that, while so simple and easy, has the power to free others from the limitations of stress and anxiety that rule their life.

There will be more books in this transformation series so keep on the lookout for the next installment in the healing journey...

A Caring and warm mother of three, Kim also enjoys speaking professionally, teaching at Workshops, Events & Community Groups.

Visit her website at: www.fastereft.net.au

Printed in Great Britain
by Amazon.co.uk, Ltd.,
Marston Gate.